With love and appreciation,
I dedicate this book to my wife,
Edith Long Schisler

Contents

Acknowledgments

Clearly, I owe a very early debt of gratitude for this book to my mama, Clara Hunkins Fry, who first made me think about Jesus.

My college professor of religion, Ed Mattingly, of Nebraska Wesleyan University, engaged my serious concern with how I would view the inescapable figure of Jesus. Late nights of discussion in a cell group led by Professor Mattingly afforded me a medium for the expression of sometimes fanciful flights of imagination while we wrestled with Gospel versus Paul issues. To Ed Mattingly, I am eternally grateful for his open spirit and patient questioning.

I am grateful as well to Keith Kenney who loaned me his copy of *Beyond Belief* by Elaine Pagels, which broke open for me at last the profound significance of the scholarly research that was well under way into the controversies among the varied groups constituting the early Jesus movement.

Jim Farrell forced me, with his incisive questioning, to reassess my intention and clarify my purpose in struggling with the ancient question: who was Jesus? His was the gift of a good friend.

Then Marilynn Peterson, a friend of many years, read the chapters one by one and enabled me to clarify my thinking and sharpen my arguments.

Beyond these influences, there are those who, in casual or even earnest conversation, have forced me to think and rethink some of the conclusions to which I have come and to which I cling. I cling to them in the expectation that they will be challenged by friends and foes alike, probably before they even finish reading these pages. I thank them in anticipation.

As always, my family has upheld me and encouraged me without fully understanding what I was up to. This has been especially true of my wife, Edith Long Schisler, whose constant love and support allowed me to move from my own self-understanding as a seeker to be what she calls, with a smile, a "rebel."

My thanks to them all.

Finally, all those mentioned above must be held blameless.

Introduction
Who Was Jesus Really?

Was Jesus a woman? She had long hair and wore a dress. I don't think I had noticed the beard. So it was a shock when my mama told me Jesus was a man. It was a lot like finding out that Santa Claus was really my father. I didn't appreciate it very much. It was very unsettling to a small child.

But what came next was worse. One day I heard that Jesus was God. That was still harder. I had just become accustomed to thinking that Jesus was a man when I had to adjust my thinking again and start viewing him as God too. I was a pretty confused little boy because I didn't know who to pray to anymore when I went to bed at night.

Then came a time when I had to face the issue in a bit more sophisticated fashion. I learned from a college professor to ask myself which view of Christian faith I was going to adopt. I could read the four Gospels and try to adopt the faith in God that Jesus manifested and taught there, or I could adopt the beliefs about who Jesus was that St. Paul proclaimed in his letters. The four Gospels of the New Testament primarily report the teachings and actions of Jesus but offer no real theories about his identity other than the belief that he was the expected Messiah of the Jews. On the other hand, the letters of Paul are primarily devoted to Jesus' identity as the only Son of God whose death was the atonement for the sins of the world and whose resurrection was the guarantee of eternal life for believers.

In other words, I could choose between the faith *of* Jesus and the faith *about* Jesus. They were two different things, and I needed to choose between them. Had I been taught the fundamentalist doctrine of the literal inspiration of the Bible, I would surely have found this suggestion intolerable. Nevertheless, I still thought it was advisable to attempt to reconcile the two approaches. For the next forty-five years I worked at it, along with another six or eight apparently irreconcilable pairs of propositions. For example, "God is one"/"God is three" and "We are saved by grace through our faith"/"Faith without works is dead."

The question about the role of Jesus in Christian faith finally came to a head for me when I was forced to face it while writing my book, *A New Vision of God for the 21st Century*. In that book, I had found it impossible to affirm two of the most important aspects of Paul's view of Jesus. They were 1) the view of Jesus as the unique (only) Son of God (Romans 1:3,4), a view only later philosophized, formalized, and promulgated by the Council of Nicea in 325 CE (meaning the "Common Era"); and 2) the view of Jesus' death as a blood atonement (Romans 5:9). So I could affirm neither the uniqueness of Jesus through his identification as the only Son of God nor his role as the blood atonement for sin. Therefore, I would have to believe something different about him.

Moreover, a nearer acquaintance with the uncertainties about the accuracy of the Jesus stories in the four Gospels made it impossible for me to take everything I found there to be informative for imitating Jesus' faith in God. So I needed to find another way to view the Gospel stories too.

Not only does the New Testament leave me with but little to go on when I come to ask who Jesus really was, but there also exists an entire library of other documents, most of which have remained hidden away in the dark places of ancient monasteries and in the desert sands of Egypt for centuries. Of course, the Church Fathers sometimes referred in their writings to those ancient documents, so modern scholars have long known that many of them once existed. But more recent discoveries have made their contents known in much fuller measure. Many of them were apparently hidden during the period when orthodoxy was in the process of being established by the church. Documents which pictured Jesus in a different manner from the views propounded in those chosen to be included in the canon of the New Testament became anathema and were burned, and their authors and possessors declared to be heretics. It was dangerous to be in possession of such documents. With their rediscovery in modern times, our picture of Jesus has just become further muddied.

The early Jesus movement, as distinguished from recent movements by the same name, was made up of many scattered groups, often with little communication among them. There was no unity in the first three centuries after Jesus' death. Geographical areas, national cultures, and religious traditions all had their unique takes on Jesus' identity and teachings. For example, Jewish groups, and later even the Muslims, had their collections of sayings attributed to Jesus. The Gnostic Christians of those early years sought salvation by esoteric knowledge, and so they also focused on Jesus' teachings. For them, Jesus was the dispenser of that "secret" knowledge or wisdom.

The recent popular mystery novel by Dan Brown, *The Da Vinci Code,* referred to the Gnostic view of Jesus as a very human teacher who was married to Mary Magdalene, with whom he had children. This tradition was affirmed by one of the novel's characters who quotes from the Gnostic *Gospel of Mary* and *Gospel of Philip* as his sources for that view. Thus, this novel has opened up to the public the whole field of diverse traditions and old disputes present in the early Jesus movement, even though it did so in the context of a piece of fiction. These facts about the period before the church took strict form have long been known to scholars.

More recently, the *Gospel of Judas* was discovered in its entirety in the 1970s, and finally translated into English in 2006. In this gospel, Judas comes off as a coconspirator with Jesus. That is, he and Jesus had planned his betrayal in advance in order to enable Jesus to die for the salvation of the world.

I have known about the existence of some of these writings, though in no detail, ever since theological school. But the significance of them for understanding the church and Jesus was never made clear to me. Therefore, my interest in them was never whetted until, while writing my book on *A New Vision of God for the 21st Century,* I read *A History of God* by Karen Armstrong and began to read about Wesley's use of the Ante-Nicene Fathers.

An understanding of the chaotic development of the early Jesus movement has enabled us to appreciate why Constantine thought the unification of that movement was necessary and that a final version of the truth about Jesus should be set forth. Therefore, the doctrine of the divinity of Jesus was promulgated at the Council of Nicea in 325

CE and the canon of the New Testament was established in the years that followed.

Nevertheless, the search for the historical Jesus has engaged serious scholars ever since Albert Schweitzer first made it respectable when he published *The Quest of the Historical Jesus* in 1906. It has been an active pursuit ever since and has recently taken on new vitality.

The discovery of ancient texts long hidden in caves, old libraries, and monasteries has been going on for years. However, new life was breathed into biblical scholarship with the discovery in 1945, at Dag Hammadi in Egypt, of a large cache of codices (bound books). The Dead Sea Scrolls, discovered in 1947, gained worldwide attention. Then, as recently as the 1970s, the Gospel of Judas was found, also in Egypt. These finds have spurred a group of somewhat popular publications devoted to the education of the public. Moreover, new archeological discoveries have added new information about the first-century Jesus movement and have produced new theories about the life of Jesus himself.[1]

Popularized treatments of recent scholarly discoveries include Bart Ehrman's *Lost Scriptures*, James Robinson's *The Gospel of Jesus*, Elaine Pagel's *Beyond Belief*, and James Tabor's *The Jesus Dynasty*. Much of the popularity of these books, however, was stimulated by Dan Brown's novel.

Nevertheless, many other books about Jesus have also been published recently in an effort to reject the conclusions of that newer scholarship and to defend traditional orthodox views. Among such books are *What Jesus Meant* by Garry Wills, *Jesus, the Final Days* by Craig Evans and N. T. Wright, *The Case for the Real Jesus* by Lee Strobel, and *Jesus of Nazareth* by Pope Benedict XVI.

For me, none of them are persuasive because they largely ignore the earliest history of the Jesus movement in favor of traditions which arose much later. So I am still left with these questions: "Who was Jesus?" Did Jesus ever live at all? Was he really born of a virgin? Did he really perform all those miracles? What was he trying to accomplish? Why did he die? Did he really come back from the dead? Was he also God? What was he really like as a historical person? What can I believe about Jesus? Who is he for me? Did he really say all the things the Bible says he did?

These old questions acquired a new urgency for me when I wrote *A New Vision of God for the 21st Century*. As a matter of fact, a new way of thinking about who God is suggested to me a new way of understanding Jesus. But I am, no doubt, almost as ignorant today about who the historical Jesus really was, what he did and said, as I was when my mama first told me that Jesus was a man. Still, I honor this man I do not know but whose story constitutes the heart of the tradition into which I was born and with which I have lived to this day. For me personally, therefore, the issue is at least seventy years old. For increasing numbers of people in the twenty-first century, the questions surrounding the person of Jesus have become acute—if the subject of Jesus has not already been simply dismissed from their consideration altogether.

At the same time, ready access to new information about the early Jesus movement has offered new possibilities for alternative ways of appropriating the Jesus stories. These two influences, my love of the tradition about Jesus (all biblical quotations are taken from the New International Version of the Bible) and recently acquired information about the early Jesus movement, have combined to guide me in the construction of a recommended way of using the stories about Jesus in the pursuit of our spiritual growth.

As I approached this task, I was aware that my entire spiritual journey had taken me along a somewhat winding pathway. Though it began in my childhood home, it continued throughout my college years and my more formal studies of theology and church history in Garrett Evangelical Theological Seminary. Five years as a missionary in Brazil interrupted those studies, though I served as a lay pastor for four of them. After finishing my seminary degree in the States, I pursued a career as a local church pastor for another thirty-four years. During those years I returned to graduate school at Rensselaer Polytechnic Institute where I took master of science and PhD degrees in philosophy. Retirement has finally afforded me the time to do the kind of further study and research that has enabled me to publish a book called *A New Vision of God for the 21st Century* and has led me to this point on that journey.

So, this book is my effort to tell you who Jesus has become for me (though his historical reality is largely lost forever), to suggest who he may be for you, and to describe how I have come to this understanding.

To do this will first require a look at the early history of the Jesus movement in chapters 1 and 2. Chapter 3 will draw the conclusions which must be drawn about the limits of our knowledge of Jesus. How the church has rewritten that history and created a religion without a firm historical foundation is the issue in chapter 4. In Part II, you will find a shift of gears from the factual, historical style of the first four chapters to a forward looking, constructive style of writing. The three chapters of Part II discuss the rationale for a new treatment of Jesus, the setting forth of a new mythic tale, and what this new image of Jesus can mean in the twenty-first century.

PART I

Chapter 1

✦

The Movement Begins

Some will be offended by the suggestion that we cannot trust everything the New Testament says about the life and ministry of Jesus. Others may have harbored the feeling that there was much there that was very problematic, for example, the miracles of healing and interference with the laws of nature. But most of the rest has gone unquestioned. Those who have further doubts about the veracity of the biblical accounts are often looked upon with great suspicion. I must say immediately, however, that I fully understand the skepticism of some and ask your patience as I seek to make clear the reasons for my suggestion. At the same time, I welcome the ready acceptance of others.

In the church we have often raised the question, without answering it, as to why the biblical learning that pastors receive in their seminary training seems to have been largely ignored when they assume their roles as pastors of churches. For example, how many parishioners have never known that the books in our New Testament, which are called "canonical," are a very small part of the literature which was produced by the early Jesus movement? Seminarians were taught that. We were also taught the history of the process by which those books were chosen to be included. But that process was rarely ever questioned, and it was much too disturbing to question it with our laymen. We had an institution to serve, as well as a congregation to protect, and perhaps we did not want to face the questions ourselves.

However, there comes a time when we must do so. As we enter the twenty-first century on the run, as it were, we are already beginning to smell the dust, and our churches are dropping farther and farther behind the world in which they are attempting to live. So I invite you to undertake, with me, an adventure that promises a new understanding and a more profound spirituality.

* * *

The name "Palestine" is the name that the Romans gave to a certain geographical area in the Middle East for purposes of governance. Most of Jesus' followers in the first generation after his death were the Jews who lived in the Palestine of the Roman occupation. They had all inherited certain expectations. Ever since the return from exile in Babylon five hundred years earlier, the Jews had experienced the occupation of their land by the Egyptians, the Greeks, and finally the Romans. By 225 BCE (signifies "before the Common Era"), they began to believe that the Day of the Lord would come, and the golden age of David would return, when the yoke of foreign oppression was cast off. They had been waiting for almost three hundred years for that day. Many charismatic personalities had appeared and were hailed as the one who was to come—a new prophet, a new king, a messiah who would deliver the people from their slavery. Jesus, almost certainly, was one of them. Matthew says he came announcing that "the Kingdom of God has come near,"[2] just as John the Baptizer had done before him

What happened in the earliest days of the Jesus movement just following the death of Jesus can best be understood in terms of Michael White's distinction between sect and cult. Of a sect he says, "A sect is a separatist, or schismatic, revitalization movement that arises out of an established religiously defined cultural system with which it shares its symbolic worldview."[3] The Jesus movement began as a Jewish sect, a part of Judaism with its own unique take on the worldview and religious tradition of Judaism which it continued to claim. White explains that since the Jesus movement continued, in the beginning, to share the Jewish worldview, it was threatened with reabsorption and consequently developed its own rhetoric which, in turn, tended to separate it from its original worldview.

But, says White, a cult differs from a sect: "A cult is an integrative, often syncretistic, movement that is effectively imported (by mobilization or mutation) into another religiously defined cultural system, to that it must seek to synthesize its novel symbolic world view."[4]

That is, a cult attempts to introduce a new world view into an existing world view. In order to do this, its followers try to soften the resulting tension by stressing the similarities between the two cultural worldviews.

Several different branches of the Jewish Jesus sect appear to have existed in Palestine during the first years after Jesus' death, though they left no written record. Paul's letters refer to those whom he calls the "judaizers." He also visited the Jewish church that still existed in Jerusalem for counsel. Roman sources also refer to them. Eventually, however, the Jesus movement began to transform itself from a Jewish sect into a Gentile (non-Jewish) or Roman cult. Central to this transformation was the adoption of Greek concepts into the explanations of Christian teachings, thus lessening the conflict between world views. This transformation had to proceed before the Jesus movement could find its own unique identity as a separate religion. The Council of Nicea in 325 CE may be seen as the terminal act of self-identification in this process.

Factors in the Transformational Process

One clue to this transformational process is seen in the contrast between the Gospel of Matthew, which probably was written for Jewish followers of Jesus soon after the destruction of the Jewish Temple in Jerusalem by the Romans in 70 CE, and the Gospel of Luke, written for Gentile followers of Jesus, perhaps in the following decade of the 80s CE. Luke's companion work, known as the "Acts of the Apostles," describes the ministry of Paul that had taken place three decades earlier in the 50s CE, when the Jesus movement was first entering the Gentile world. Therefore, Paul was already planting the seeds as the Jesus movement began to change from sect to cult.

Much of what we can guess about Jesus has been deduced from our knowledge of the time in which he lived. For instance, we know that Aramaic was the common language of the people in Jesus' day. It was a cognate of ancient Hebrew and had been the language of the Jews since the Babylonian captivity.[5] Thus, we can be sure that Jesus spoke Aramaic. Did he also know Greek? Possibly, if he had worked with his father in the construction of the Greek city of Sepphoris over on a hilltop near Nazareth. But there is no evidence of that. Did he know Hebrew? Not likely. It was the language of the learned in the law, and there is no reason to think Jesus was one of them. Most of the common people, in fact, were illiterate. Was Jesus illiterate?

It is also pretty clear that Jesus' compatriots would have been asking whether or not he was the coming deliverer, the true herald and precursor of The day of the Lord. Those who followed him were either convinced or wanted to be. Furthermore, they believed that deliverance was imminent. The Day was at hand. This expectation is known as the "apocalyptic hope." It promised that a theistic God would one day intervene in the affairs of the nations to strike the yoke of Rome off the necks of the Jews.

However, many had wanted to take things into their own hands. More than once, violent rebellions had broken out. The Zealots of Jesus' time were still fomenting revolution, but mixed in with the rebellion was the apocalyptic hope. Jesus, like many before him, probably expected the coming of the Kingdom in some form. Therefore, the followers of Jesus would have constituted a movement within Judaism. Jesus may have been put to death primarily by the Romans in the interest of peace in the land—perhaps because, confusing the two, they might have taken his apocalyptic message as a call for revolution.

We also know that in Roman culture, which in some ways had replaced Greek culture, the gods were rejected and the ruling religious duty was to imitate the natural law of God. Their idea of God, however, was what the historian, Williston Walker, characterizes as "pantheistic monotheism.[6] That is, God was identified with the natural world in which one could find his will embedded. Thus the Jewish worldview, and at least initially that of Jesus, was fundamentally at odds with the world view of the Gentiles. In Rome the embodiment of God was the emperor. Therefore, in Palestine, the seeds of conflict between worldviews were already germinating in Jesus' world.

All this, of course, is a common sense view of the situation derived primarily from our knowledge of Jewish history. It is not precisely the picture we receive from reading the four gospel accounts of Jesus' life and ministry in the New Testament, but that is understandable in view of the fact that those accounts were each written more than forty years after Jesus' death by non-contemporaries. Moreover, two of the four gospels were clearly written by non-Jewish persons, and each of them has its own perspective and unique purpose because all were written after the fall of Jerusalem and the destruction of the Temple in 70 CE.

In fact, many scholars today believe the development of most of the earliest Christian literature, some of which had found its way into the New Testament by the end of the fourth century CE, may be traced to the impact of the failure of the apocalyptic hope. And that failure was widely identified with the failure of the rebellion that resulted in Jerusalem's fall. So how did that event come to occur?

Following Jesus' death, the Roman Empire was already in a boil. The Jews never had been comfortable under Roman rule, and the hope of freedom now drove the fledgling Jesus movement. When Paul began his ministry, twenty years had passed since Jesus' death and things were beginning to churn dangerously. The Jews had a reputation for being an obstreperous people. Many years before, Syria, and then Rome, had to put down rebellions led by the Maccabees, and there was always someone or other to stir up the people, raise arms, and threaten to attack Rome again. Followers of Jesus, who were seen as Jews gone mad, had come under pressure from Rome, and occasional outbursts of persecution had taken place in the empire. But before the unrest erupted into open rebellion, Paul showed up on the scene.

Paul's Role in the Separation from Judaism

So what about Paul? Clearly his letters were written prior to the ill-fated Jewish revolt and also prior to the writing of the gospel accounts recorded in the New Testament. I'm guessing he may have despaired, from the beginning of his ministry, of the success of any armed rebellion against Rome. But, as a good apocalyptist, he all but ignored Jesus as a teacher and treated him almost exclusively as the herald and executor of the coming Kingdom of God. Early in his career, Paul's moral teachings focused on the Old Testament law, which was to be obeyed in the Spirit rather than to the letter. Almost no attention is given to anything Jesus said. So far, the law had served as a disciplinarian,[7] but now, Paul says, "The only thing that counts is faith working through love." This is not the way Jesus likely would have talked about it, but we shall see that it may not be very different from what we may tentatively assume Jesus to have taught.

For Paul, the Kingdom was not reserved for Israel, but belonged to the Gentile world as well. In Romans he writes the following:

I am talking to you Gentiles. … If the part of the dough that is offered as first fruits is holy, then the whole batch is holy; if the root is holy, so are the branches.[8]

Moreover, his interpretation of the coming Kingdom was otherworldly. It was "not a matter of eating and drinking, but of righteousness, peace and joy in the Holy Spirit."[9]

He took the historicity of Jesus seriously, but not the content of his life and teaching. Not even his birth counted for anything. Primarily, his death and resurrection were seen as the occasions of his messianic work. Of course, he does attribute righteousness to Jesus, but it was the righteousness defined either by obedience to the law or by Jesus' obedience to God in going to the cross.

Of the twenty-seven documents in our New Testament, twenty-two were written either wholly or partially in letter form. Letters were the primary form of literary communication in those times.[10] Of the letters traditionally attributed to Paul, there is still debate about the authorship of Ephesians, Colossians, and 2 Thessalonians. It is highly doubtful that Paul wrote 1 Timothy, 2 Timothy, and Titus. Hebrews was not written by him. The seven letters now attributed with certitude to Paul's authorship are Romans, 1 Corinthians, 2 Corinthians, Galatians, Philippians, 1 Thessalonians, and Philemon. In them, I find only the broadest hints that Paul may have had some acquaintance with the traditions about Jesus' teaching. For example, here is a quick look at a few of Paul's letters. You may want to take your own look at the rest of the letters that are securely assigned to Paul.

1 Thessalonians (50–51 CE)

The earliest of his known letters was 1 Thessalonians, written circa 50–51 CE.[11] Paul's first reference to Jesus speaks of

your work produced by faith, your labor prompted by love, and your endurance inspired by hope in our Lord Jesus Christ … they tell how you turned to God from idols, to serve the living and true God, and to wait for his Son from Heaven, whom he raised from the dead—Jesus, who rescues us from the coming wrath..[11]

There is no word about Jesus' teaching—only about his coming from heaven.

Paul also says,

You became imitators of us and of the Lord.[12]

Now we ask and urge you in the Lord Jesus to do this more and more. For you know what instruction we gave you by the authority of the Lord Jesus.[13]

His readers were to imitate Paul and Jesus in the way they lived until Jesus came from heaven. But just what that means is unclear. Does this suggest that Paul's readers were already well acquainted with Jesus' teachings? Or is he implying that by imitating him (Paul), they are also imitating the Lord Jesus, thus learning their behavior from Paul's example rather than from Jesus' teachings? Is that why he doesn't quote anything from Jesus?

There are a few exhortations to love one another, but never a word quoting Jesus' teachings. It seems highly likely that he intends to head in another direction altogether. The Gospel, which literally means "good news," of the Lord of which he writes is clearly the apocalyptic hope.

For the Lord himself will come down from heaven, and with a loud command, with the voice of the archangel and the trumpet call of God, and the dead in Christ will rise first. After that we who are still alive and are left will be caught up together with them in the clouds to meet the Lord. And so we will be with the Lord forever.[14]

This is Paul's message to the Jesus people in Thessalonika. There is an urgency here that seems to diminish with the later letters, but is still present in increasingly modified form and with a more individualized content.

1 Corinthians (53–54 CE)

Paul's first letter to the Corinthians was the next of the seven letters to be written. Once again, the promise is that

> *he will keep you strong to the end, so that you will be blameless on the day of our Lord Jesus Christ.*[15]

That day has been guaranteed by Jesus' death on the cross and his resurrection. His cross as "the wisdom of God" is compared to the "wisdom of the world," which is powerless.

> *For Christ did not send me to baptize but to preach the gospel, not with words of human wisdom, lest the cross of Christ be emptied of its power.*[16]

Then he quotes Hebrew scripture, not Jesus:

> *I will destroy the wisdom of the wise; the intelligence of the intelligent I will frustrate.*[17]

There was another tune (Gnosticism) within the Jesus movement that a little later began to exercise great influence. In that movement, the life and teachings of Jesus were considered to be the wisdom of God. Whether that movement had begun to raise its head in Paul's time is not known.[18] However, it appears that the wisdom of God, which Paul says Jesus became, had nothing to do with Jesus' teachings, but rather with the claim that his death and resurrection were themselves the wisdom of God. Of course, they were wisdom only in the sense that they were God's substitute for the wisdom of the world, and somehow that wisdom was the source of every blessing.

> *It is because of him that you are in Christ Jesus, who has become for us wisdom from God that is, our righteousness, holiness and redemption.*[19]

It seems possible that Paul had heard some of the sayings of Jesus from others, but decided to deliberately ignore them simply because he had a different theory about the significance of Jesus. It is hard not to assume this was the case. In fact, he also speaks of the wisdom of God a little differently as he moves through this letter.

> *No, we speak God's secret wisdom that has been hidden and that*
> *God destined for our glory before time began.*[20]

Here God's wisdom seems to be something he speaks or announces rather than something Jesus' has done. Perhaps Paul assumes that both the reality of Jesus death and resurrection, and the announcement of that good news, are simply different forms of God's wisdom. However, the gifts and guidance of the Holy Spirit are also cited as sources of God's wisdom. Whatever Paul was thinking, we still have nothing from the mouth of Jesus and, therefore, his view of wisdom remains confused.

So, I look through this important letter of Paul's and never find a single teaching from the lips of Jesus himself. However, Paul's message of death and resurrection is proclaimed in verse after verse. Just take a look at the following verses in 1 Corinthians: 2:12–13; 3:11; 5:7b; 6:11; and 6:20.

In chapter 7 through the end of the letter, one finds a wealth of wise advice from Paul, but again, never a citation of Jesus' teachings.

There is one historical reference to Jesus, however, besides his indisputable death. It is found in 11:23, and tells the story about Jesus breaking the bread and serving the cup on the night before he was killed.

> *For I received from the Lord what I also passed: the Lord Jesus,*
> *on the night he was betrayed, took bread —.*

Of course, this event could be used neatly in reinforcement of his focus on the death of Jesus. He says the Lord told him about it, but clearly he did not hear the story from the historical Jesus. One may choose to assume that he meant that he had heard it from the resurrected Jesus on the road to Damascus. However, the story of that encounter is found in Luke's Gospel, not in Paul's own account of his conversion. It is probable that he heard it from someone else, perhaps James or Peter, on his first visit to Jerusalem, which was at least three years after his conversion. If that is the case, he likely heard a good deal more about Jesus' teachings than he reveals in his letters and simply chose to ignore them because they did not fit his scheme of things.

You may want to search the other letters of Paul to discover how much he knew about the Jesus who had died twenty to twenty-five years before he wrote his letters. Presently, I want to take a look only at the last letter he wrote. Paul's letter to the Romans is the most complete treatment of his message. Maybe we will find there something that we don't find in the earlier, and shorter, letters. Certainly he developed the "benefits of his passion" most fully in Romans

Romans (58–59 CE)

Here's how Paul begins:

regarding his Son, who as to his human nature was a descendent of David, and who through the spirit of holiness was declared with power to be the Son of God by his resurrection from the dead: Jesus Christ our Lord.[21]

Here he uses Jesus' resurrection as certification of his role as Messiah or Christ (the Greek word for "Messiah"), as well as his membership in the lineage of David (an old Jewish tradition about the Messiah who was to come.).

In order to set forth the reason why all this is necessary, he harks back to the Day of Wrath, of which he wrote in 1 Thessalonians:

But because of your stubbornness and your unrepentant heart, you are storing up wrath against yourself for the day of God's wrath, when his righteous judgment will be revealed. God will give to each person according to what he has done.[22]

But why should the Gentiles be found guilty when they had never heard the Law of Moses? Paul goes on to explain why he can call them to repentance in anticipation of the coming Day of Wrath:

The wrath of God is revealed from heaven against all the godlessness and wickedness of men who suppress the truth by their wickedness, since what may be known about God is plain to them, because God has made it plain to them. For since the creation of the world God's invisible qualities—his eternal power and divine nature—have been clearly seen, being understood from what has been made, so that men are without excuse.[23]

11

The Gentiles had not stored up wrath by disobeying the Law of Moses, like the Jews had, but by committing all the kinds of immorality that Paul describes in chapter two.

Next, Paul describes the cure for the wrath that both Jews and Gentiles have stored up. They are justified (read "forgiven") because of the righteousness of Jesus Christ:

God presented him as a sacrifice of atonement, through faith in his blood.[24]

For us, to whom God will credit righteousness... He was delivered over to death for our sins and was raised to life for our justification.[25]

Paul himself seems to provide the basis for the doctrine of "substitutionary atonement," which implies that Jesus had perfectly obeyed either the Law of Moses or God's command to go to the cross, and that his obedience could be credited to the believer's moral account. For Paul, there seems to be a transfer of Jesus' righteousness to the sinner's account. That is, he says that faith in the atonement is "credited" to the believer as righteousness and, thus, one is saved from God's wrath.[26] The doctrine of "substitutionary atonement" itself asserts that Jesus was crucified as a substitute for all the sinners of the world so that they would not have to be punished for their own sins. It was a later working out of Paul's statements on atonement and eventually became the foundational doctrine of the church.

Here the righteousness associated with Jesus' death in 1 Thessalonians is more fully discussed, and once more, it has nothing to do with any teachings Jesus might have given to his followers. It is not clear that it even has anything to do with his obedience to the Law of Moses or any reported acts of mercy he might have performed. This appears to leave only Jesus' obedience to God's order to submit himself to the cross as constituting his righteousness. But Paul also writes of God "handing him over" to die on the cross, which takes all the credit away from Jesus. All we can be sure about here is that Paul simply had no use for any teachings of Jesus. Yet, even before Paul came along, soldiers in the Roman armies had been hearing reports of the words this Jewish teacher had spoken to his followers. The upshot of Paul's work was (1) a de-emphasis on the life and teachings of Jesus, and (2) a serious modification of the apocalyptic hope.

Not only did Jesus' death produce justification, or pardon, but it also produced sanctification or holiness, according to Paul. The problem Paul had been facing ever since he began his preaching was what to do about sin after one had been justified. Well, Paul spends a good deal of the rest of his letter to the Romans struggling with this issue. First, he tries to deal with it through the symbolism of dying and being raised with Christ as a new man.

> *What are we to say then? Shall we go on sinning so that grace may increase? By no means! ... We were buried with him through baptism into death in order that, just as Christ was raised from the dead through the glory of the Father, we too may live a new life.*[27]

Thus, the believer who has been pardoned is expected to be baptized, not only with the symbolic use of water, but also by dying spiritually to sin so that he might be raised free from sin. Again, Jesus' death and resurrection are the focus of all Paul's efforts to understand who Jesus was and why he was important.

A few verses later he tries something a little different. He tries to distinguish between the flesh and the spirit.

> *For what the law was powerless to do in that it was weakened by the sinful nature, God did by sending his own Son in the likeness of sinful man to be a sin offering. And so he condemned sin in sinful man, in order that the righteous requirements of the law might be fully met in us, we do not live according to the sinful nature but according to the Spirit. Those who live according to the sinful nature have their minds set on what that sinful nature desires; but those who live according to the Spirit have their minds set on what the Spirit desires. The mind of sinful man is death, but the mind controlled by the Spirit is life and peace.*[28]

So both Jews and Gentiles are given a chance to receive not only pardon, but also to live by the Spirit (holiness). However, one's conduct is still to be in accordance with the Law of Moses, not the teachings of Jesus. For this to happen, admits Paul, the discipline of the believer to set his mind on the things of the Spirit is required.

In Romans 12, Paul describes this new life in Christ, but Jesus himself is not cited, even though much of the chapter could be an echo of teachings Paul may have heard from Peter or James. The chapter ends with an exhortation which sounds like Jesus, but Paul appears to quote it as coming from the scripture, that is, the Old Testament:

> *It is written …, 'Do not be overcome by evil, but overcome evil with good.*[29]

However, this advice also may have been based on Jesus' advice, which appears in Matthew 5:38. Of course, Paul did not read it in Matthew, as it was probably not written for another twenty-five years. It is possible that it was one of the sayings that were passed on orally through the years, but were written down only much later.

Later yet, in Romans 13:6–7a, Paul may also have been depending on an oral tradition which has Jesus advising to give to Caesar what is Caesar's and to God what is God's.

More likely, this was one of the accommodations to the Roman worldview that Paul was willing to make in the movement from Jewish sect to Roman cult.

Nevertheless, he is quite clear that God's will is not something we learn from knowing what Jesus said or did. For he says,

> *Do not conform any longer to the pattern of this world, but be transformed by the renewing of your mind. Then you will be able to test and approve what God's will is—his good, pleasing and perfect will.*[30]

In other words, Paul counsels a spiritual transformation through which the will of God can be known. Perhaps, when he defines love as the "fulfilling of the Law" in the next chapter, he is assuming that the transformation of which he speaks produces the love, which somehow fulfills the law.

A bit later, Paul seems to be defining the will of God as whatever proceeds from faith:

> *"Everything that does not come from faith is sin."*[31]

But faith in what? Presumably, he means faith in what he calls "the proclamation of Jesus Christ," which he identifies as his own gospel.[32]

This would mean that whatever proceeds from faith in the atoning death of Jesus and in his resurrection is righteousness.

So, he is still ignoring the teachings of Jesus and doesn't even refer us to the Law of Moses.

Please don't think that I'm chastising Paul for refusing to cite the words of Jesus. The facts are as follows:

- He had no personal firsthand acquaintance with the historical figure of Jesus.
- No written account of Jesus' life and teachings had yet been produced.
- At best, he had no more than hearsay about Jesus' teachings,
- He had only a few bare facts to go on, such as he was a Jewish man, he announced the coming of the Kingdom of God, he died, and he was buried (1 Corinthians 15).
- After his conversion he had gone immediately to Arabia and had talked to no one else for three years before beginning his ministry. He seems to have come up with a theory about Jesus all by himself.
- Later, he may have heard some teachings of Jesus from James and Peter in Jerusalem.
- There was a tradition, only recently uncovered by modern archeologists, that had the Messiah rising from the dead on the third day, about which he may have heard.
- He was faced with a Gentile world which operated out of a different worldview.
- He had to construct a message which would speak to Gentiles, somehow including them in the promises of Israel.
- He discovered early on that the old Jewish apocalyptic hope had to be reinterpreted.
- He did the best he could do to recommend this Jesus he had somehow experienced.

Lacking information about the historical figure, but believing at least that Jesus had an apocalyptic message, Paul was able to reinterpret it in terms of two things, the prophecies of Isaiah and Jeremiah, and the death and resurrection of Jesus.

Thus, while Paul is in the process of taking the Jesus movement from Jewish sect to Gentile cult, Paul's language still places his outlook on his experience entirely within a Jewish self-understanding.[33]

I admire Paul, but he brings me no closer to the Jesus who walked the dusty roads of Roman Palestine.

He does, though, presage an early break from Judaism as the Jesus movement continued to spread throughout the known world. That is not to say he was the first to move out. There were already communities of Gentile Jesus people in Antioch, Alexandria, Rome, and other parts of the empire. He was neither the founder of the church, nor the first "Christian," but he did give impetus to the break with Judaism which soon followed.[34]

Apostles Were Eyewitnesses

Paul thought it important to establish his authority as an apostle because, by the time he became active, the first disciples of Jesus had come to be treated as the only ones who could speak with any authority. He treated his experience on the way to Damascus as the act by which the Lord gave him the same authority to speak as the disciples had. However, it was Luke, not Paul, who described the experience as a dramatic vision. Paul had simply written in his letter to the Galatians:

> *You have heard of my previous way of life in Judaism ... But when God, who set me apart from birth and called me by his grace, was pleased to reveal his Son in me so that I might preach him among the Gentiles, I did not consult any man, nor did I go up to Jerusalem to see those who were apostles before I was, but I went immediately to Arabia and later returned to Damascus.[35]*

However, Luke attributes the following description to Paul himself:

> *"About noon as I came near Damascus, suddenly a bright light from heaven flashed around me. I fell to the ground and heard a voice say to me, 'Saul! Saul! Why do you persecute me?' 'Who are you, Lord?' I asked. 'I am Jesus of Nazareth, whom you are persecuting,' he replied."[36]*

So, one wonders who elaborated the account in Acts, Paul himself in conversation with the author of Acts, or the author who wrote his account at least twenty years after Paul had died in Rome. In either case, we know Paul regarded himself as having even greater authority than did Peter who had actually known Jesus personally. Surely Peter knew better than Paul what the mind of Jesus was. Even so, Paul was able to summon up enough courage to castigate Peter, one of the early disciples of Jesus, for his confused understanding of the gospel.[37]

This incident reflects wider opposition to Paul's version of the faith as well. Here he had attacked Peter and the Galatians for continuing to obey Jewish ceremonial law concerning table fellowship with Gentiles. Paul always had to contend with those who still insisted that Gentiles had to become practicing Jews before becoming followers of Jesus. This is because Paul's view of Jesus' ministry was that he had died and risen again so that both Jews and Gentiles might live by faith and not under the law. Already, the authority of the earliest witnesses was being challenged. And we must remember that Peter, as a Jesus-following Jew, did not yet see himself as anything but a member of a Jewish sect. He lived in the earliest days of the struggle of the Jesus movement to separate itself from Judaism as a distinct religion in its own right.

Paul's ministry also encountered opposition from another direction. At least by the middle of the second century, some of the bishops of the church claimed their authority had come directly to them through the laying on of hands in direct succession from Jesus through the apostles—implying a rejection of Paul's authority.

As we have seen, the teachings of Jesus and the events in his life, apart from the passion story, were either unknown to Paul or deliberately ignored. It is no wonder that he was regarded with suspicion by many in the Jesus movement. Not only did he largely ignore the life and teachings of Jesus, but after his early teaching about the Day of Wrath, reflected in his description written to the Thessalonians, he had revised the way in which he taught about the apocalyptic hope itself.[38]

Ignoring the inconsistencies and confusions in Paul's letters, I think we may collapse his teachings into the following summation. Paul taught 1) that the new age of the Spirit, which had been introduced into history by the death and resurrection of Jesus, replaced the old age of the Law of Moses; 2) that holiness was now to be the result of one's new life in the Spirit which produces the fruits of the Spirit, righteousness, peace, joy, etc.; and finally 3) that the resurrection was the guarantee that those who experience new life in the Spirit would ascend into heaven at the last.

You can see that Paul had gradually revised the apocalyptic hope and, perhaps in anticipation of the fall of Jerusalem but more likely in the interests of accommodating the different worldview of the Gentile culture, fostered a kind of "realized eschatology." In other words, the apocalypse had already occurred.

Paul's devotion to preaching to the Gentiles pulled severely at the bonds which the early Christian Jews felt with their religious inheritance. He still believed in the coming of the Kingdom, but it was a kingdom in which deliverance was by faith and not the law. Moreover, it was not a kingdom of flesh and blood, but one of righteousness, joy, and peace.

Nevertheless, Paul was seen by the Romans as one of the hated Jewish sect that had come to be known as Christians. So he was eventually executed in Rome sometime between 62 and 64 CE. Peter suffered a similar fate. James, the brother of Jesus and leader of the Jesus movement in Jerusalem, had already been executed in Jerusalem in 61 CE. The persecution of Christians by the Romans was sporadic initially and only became severe after Paul began to sound his message of impending doom. No doubt the Romans had difficulty distinguishing between Paul's message about the Kingdom and that of the earliest Jewish Christians whose understanding of Jesus' message was different. Hence, the execution of James. But there is no biblical account of the unsettling events that were transpiring in Palestine beginning at about the time of Paul's death.

We know from other sources, however, that they were tumultuous years in Jerusalem as apocalyptic expectations and revolutionary sentiments mounted, finally catapulting Judea into open rebellion against Rome.[39]

Already the first generation of Jesus people was disappearing, and the rebellion against Rome was gaining momentum.

Chapter 2

✦

The First Great Split

The first great split occurred when the Jesus movement left its Jewish roots and became an independent religion, a process that was effectively complete by 100 CE. It had its beginning in 50 CE when Paul made his first trip to Jerusalem to consult with James and the Jewish Christians there. It was during this time that they decided that Gentile followers of Jesus didn't have to be circumcised like the Jewish followers of Jesus had been. It has also been called the "First Ecumenical Council."

However, the division was given a major push when, in 64 CE, Rome burned and Nero blamed the Christians. (The name "Christian" was first used in Antioch around the same time.) Meanwhile, word had reached Rome that a revolutionary spirit was abroad in Judea. Rioting continued to worsen through 67 CE. Josephus called the rioters "the assassins." They were not motivated primarily by the apocalyptic hope, of course, but were highly influenced by the Zealots' rebel movement. Remember that the apocalyptic hope was God's definitive intervention in history to save the people of Israel from their oppression. It did not necessarily call for a human revolution.

The Turning Point

So the revolt against Rome was now under way and would continue through 74 CE. Jewish leaders were arrested, and troops from Caesarea briefly occupied Jerusalem. The Roman governor of Syria, Cestius, called for help from Rome. Rome's response, under Vespasian, involved a campaign through Galilee toward Jerusalem. In Samaria, the Romans massacred worshippers in Gerazim. The Essenes from Qumran set out in the belief that this was the great battle between dark and light. They too were massacred, but the campaign underwent a delay when the Emperor Nero was murdered in Rome.

During this lull, Jewish rebels took courage, believing it was due to the intervention of God. But when Vespasian became emperor following the murder of Nero, his son Titus took up the delayed siege of Jerusalem. He laid siege from the hills surrounding the city, thus cutting it off from all aid and food supplies from the outside. Famine ran rampant. On September 20 in 70 CE, Titus entered Jerusalem. The revolt had failed and the Temple and the holy city were ravaged.

Michael White sums up the situation in his book, *From Jesus to Christianity,* "The event sent shock waves through the Jewish population both in the homeland and in the Diaspora (the Jews who had scattered to lands outside the holy land). Josephus reports a total of 1.1 million casualties, mostly Jewish, and 97,000 Jews were taken prisoner. The loss of life was devastating to be sure, but the destruction of Jerusalem and especially the Temple—symbol of the nation and of God's election—was even more devastating politically, economically, and emotionally."[40]

What did this disaster mean? Where were the sacrifices to be made? How could Jews continue to observe their feasts and holy days? How could the nations ever come to the Holy Hill when it had been laid waste? The whole structure of Jewish faith and the hope in which the people had been living, at least since the third century BCE, were in shambles.

Not only were traditional Jews shaken, but Jesus followers, Jewish as well as Gentile, who had continued to expect the coming of the Kingdom of God, also came under tremendous pressure to explain what had happened and to recreate the hope which had sustained them for so long.

The upshot of this unexpected outcome was a desperate attempt by everyone to justify the hope by reinterpreting it—by moving the expected victory further into the future or by revising the picture of what the expected Kingdom would look like.

Therefore, this entire period in Jewish history represents a time of reformation. Two major branches grew out of the failure of hope. One is called "rabbinic Judaism," or the rabbinic movement, which took shape largely in Galilee where many Jews had fled. It was a concerted effort within Judaism to reinterpret the hope and adjust itself to the fall of Jerusalem and the destruction of the Temple. A rabbinic work known as the Mishna, also called the "second Torah," was prompted by this failure. The movement informs Judaism to this day. Contemporary Judaism is characterized by diverse segments, each with its own unique response.

The other branch springing from these disastrous times was that of the Jewish followers of Jesus who rejected the rabbinic movement and formed themselves into a group known as the Ebionites, which, in Aramaic, meant "the poor." This name probably came from the beatitude blessing "the poor," which is first found in a hypothetical document called Q.[41] This early, missing countercultural document was probably produced between 50 and 60 CE, contemporaneously with Paul's letters. If so, the Jewish followers of Jesus who became the Ebionites may have been familiar with the Q document and its revised view of the apocalypse. Thus, they would have been prepared for the disaster of Jerusalem's fall.

Christian Gnosticism

By the time Paul's churches and the Ebionite churches surfaced and were contending for dominance, there had arisen another movement among the Jesus followers. It was called "Gnosticism." It threatened nearly all of the contentions of the Pauline segment and some aspects of the Jewish branch of the movement as well. Its origin was attributed to a mysterious figure known as Simon Magus (the magician), but nothing is known of him. Neither is it known if it was originally a non-Christian movement which later adopted Jesus as its main teacher, nor if it arose as part of the Jesus movement itself. The Gnostic Christians of those early years sought salvation by esoteric knowledge, and so they also focused on Jesus' teachings. For them, Jesus was the dispenser of that knowledge or wisdom. Gnosticism became a major contender for dominance in the Jesus movement about the time when the split with Judaism had gained full force.

The Gnostics' view of Jesus, as the bearer of a new kind of wisdom, came from Docetism,[42] which was, in turn, borrowed from Plato's vision of the world as a shadow of the real world of ideas. The whole structure of Plato's teaching rested on the notion that what is real are the ideas which reside in the spiritual realm, or in God. For example, the idea of "chair" is the reality, while the many chairs in the natural world are representatives or "shadows" of the real idea. Thus, the natural world is constituted of shadows of those ideas which inhabited the mind of God.

Plato's most famous treatment of this notion is found in his dialogue called *The Republic*. There he tells the story of a person sitting in a cave with his back to the entrance, looking at the back wall of the cave. This person sees the shadows cast by the sun as it shines on the real world of ideas and projects their shadows through the entrance onto the back wall. The observer sees only the shadows and assumes they are the real world.

Docetism was the philosophical movement that took Plato's notion and claimed the natural world only "appeared" to be real. The Gnostics, in turn, took this idea and adapted it to their teaching about Jesus who, they claimed, only appeared to be a real human being who thirsted on the cross and died there. But he was, in fact, a spiritual reality who could neither thirst nor die. Therefore, his teachings, when obeyed, would lead believers to understand that they were really spiritual beings like Jesus and would, thus, achieve salvation. For this reason, they ran into conflict both with the early Jewish followers and with the Paul-influenced Christians who became the orthodox believers. (These orthodox believers should not be confused with the Eastern Orthodox Church which didn't come into existence until circa 1000 CE.) There was more to Gnosticism than is described above, but that was the basis of it.

Though called esoteric or mystical, its teachings were obliquely set forth in the Gnostic writings, one of which was the Gospel of Thomas. Besides Thomas, there were other Gnostic gospels written during the second half of the first century and on into the early fourth century CE, such as the Gospels of Mary, Philip, and The Truth.

Unfortunately, our modern church histories tend to play down the significance of large segments of the early Jesus movement. For example, Williston Walker, in his book, *A History of the Christian Church*, has a chapter called "From the Gnostic Crisis to Constantine." He called it a "crisis" because he viewed the movement as an intrusion into "the church" which he assumed already existed. The fact is that the Gentile focus which we have described was itself an intrusion into the original version which emphasized the teachings and life of Jesus.

Even so, it was no less an intrusion than was the later importation of Greek concepts into the Gentile church in its development of doctrinal orthodoxy. All talk about orthodoxy or the orthodox church as the original or the norm, or even the majority, is clearly misguided. The original was the Jewish Jesus sect.

Gnostic Christianity was naturally seen by the orthodox as a crisis because it focused on the teachings of Jesus almost exclusively, effectively ignoring the doctrinal accretions fomented by Paul and later fixed in the orthodoxy of the church. Therefore, from the point of view of the Gnostic Christians, Paul's version, and that of some of the most vocal bishops, was itself a disaster and was seen as a crisis for Gnostic teachings. In the Gnostic document called the Apocalypse of Peter, the author attacks, "those who call themselves bishops and deacons as though they had received their authority from God ... (but are) dry canals."[43]

Paul's concern with the "wisdom of the world" might have been his response to Gnostic claims that they possessed the saving wisdom. If so, this would place the origin of Gnosticism early in the first century CE, before Paul wrote. However, most scholars place its origin later in the century. So we may assume the wisdom against which Paul inveighed was the teachings the Jewish Jesus movement valued so greatly.

Fallout from the Disaster

Close on the heels of the big failure of the apocalyptic message, there appeared the first known written story of Jesus' life and ministry. It was subsequently given the name of "Mark," with only the slightest justification.

It was written in Greek, apparently for Gentile followers of Jesus, as an effort to preserve something of their history and tradition in view of the devastation suffered by the fall of Jerusalem in 70 CE. After all, the apocalyptic hope of many of the Gentile Christians was still connected with Jerusalem and its Temple due to Paul's teaching. However, what is now called the "Sayings Gospel Q" (see above reference to Q) arose from and was directed to the Jewish followers of Jesus.

So what is this hypothetical Q document?

The hypothesis that there existed a document containing a collection of the sayings of Jesus is derived from a singular fact about two later gospels, Matthew and Luke. Scholars early on had noticed that many of the sayings reported in both Matthew and Luke were nearly identical and appeared in nearly the same order in both stories. However, none of these sayings appear in Mark. On the other hand, both Matthew and Luke appeared to be using Mark for their information about the order of events in Jesus' life. Therefore, the scholars concluded both Mathew and Luke had used Mark and some other written source for their accounts. The other source, being hypothetical, was called Q. Though written in Greek, the original sayings of Jesus were, of course, spoken in Aramaic.

The Gospel of Thomas was discovered in 1945 at Nag Hammadi in Egypt, but probably dates from this same early period. This gospel originated in the Gnostic Christian community, which was, by then, vying for dominance in the early Jesus movement. Only after the discovery of the full text in Coptic, an early Egyptian cognate language, was it discovered that fragments of Thomas in Greek had already come to light circa 1900.

Since the full text of this gospel is now available, we know that many of the Q sayings were also included in Thomas. In fact, scholar Elaine Pagels believes that Thomas may have been in contention with the Gospel of John for inclusion when the New Testament canon was finally established in the end of the fourth century CE. One may suspect why Thomas was not included. First, it totally ignored the death and resurrection of Jesus. Second, its focus was almost entirely on the sayings of Jesus, which was typical of both the earliest Jesus followers and the Christian Gnostic movement that had arisen sometime during the first century CE. Forty-eight passages from the Q document appear in the Gospel of Thomas.[44]

The Gospel of Thomas has been characterized by Michael Whitre as follows: "The eschatology is thoroughly spiritualized or 'realized' and Jesus speaks as a heavenly figure—with the voice of Wisdom (Sophia)—giving instructions to those who are presently in the divine kingdom ... More striking is the fact that there is no reference to Jesus' death, burial and resurrection. Instead, the figure of Jesus has Docetic features that are symbolized in the idea of 'twinship'—in which the human believer is symbolized by Thomas the twin, and the living Jesus is an entirely spiritual image to be emulated. He is the inner spiritual light."[45]

One example of the apocalyptic material believed to have been derived from Q may be seen by comparing Luke and Matthew , though it does not appear in Thomas.

John said to the crowds coming to be baptized by him, "You brood of vipers! Who warned you to flee from the coming wrath? Produce fruit in keeping with repentance. And do not begin to say to yourselves, 'We have Abraham as our father!' For I tell you that out of these stones God can raise up children for Abraham. The ax is already at the root of the trees, and every tree that does not produce good fruit will be cut down and thrown into the fire."

—Luke 3:7–9

But when he saw many of the Pharisees and Sadducees coming to where he was baptizing, he said to them: "You brood of vipers! Who warned you to flee from the coming wrath? Produce fruit in keeping with repentance. And do not think you can say to yourselves, 'We have Abraham as our father.' I tell you that out of these stones God can raise up children for Abraham The ax is already at the root of the trees, and every tree that does not produce good fruit will be cut own and thrown into the fire."

—Matthew 3:7–10

The expression "the coming wrath" in Q seems at first to be a reference to the traditional expectation of God's radical intervention. The text, however, seems to imply that the "day of wrath," in its original sense, is not what they needed to fear. Rather, for Q, the warning to the "brood of vipers" is directed toward the crowds and/or the authorities who reject Jesus' teachings.

The "brood of vipers" appears in both Luke and Matthew, but not in Thomas, perhaps because Thomas took it to refer to the traditional intervention of God. Matthew and Luke wanted to cite it because it gave both of them an excuse to focus on the passion story and their own Pauline view of the apocalypse.

The theme of the Kingdom of God runs through it all. Of course. James Robinson, translator of the "Sayings Gospel Q" and perhaps its leading authority, suggests that, in view of the way "Kingdom of God" is used in Q, it would be more accurate to speak of "God reigning."

That is, the Kingdom of God should be understood as an action, not as a state of things. Given this interpretation, we can already see how Jesus may have been revising the apocalyptic hope.

For example, the following passage from Q, which is found in all three gospels, paints a very different picture of the Kingdom.

> *Once, having been asked by the Pharisees when the kingdom of God would come, Jesus replied, "The kingdom of God does not come with your careful observation, nor will people say, 'Here it is,' or 'There it is,' because the kingdom of God is within you."*

—Luke 17:20–21

> *At that time, if anyone says to you, "'Look, here is the Christ!" or "There he is!" do not believe it.*

—Matthew 24:23

The version in Luke also shows up in Thomas 3:1–3 and 113.

Since the Luke/Thomas version is very compatible with Gnostic views of the Kingdom, and Luke usually does less editing of the material from Q than Matthew does, we may assume it is probably the most faithful to Q. After all, Luke seems to be in the process of discounting the countercultural sayings of Q anyway, so he would have less interest in editing it. Matthew would not be interested in forwarding the Gnostic-sounding clause "the Kingdom of God is within you," so apparently edited it out. And for Thomas, the Kingdom is already within those who trust God reigning and observe the teachings of Jesus.

The Q scholar, James Robinson, observes of the earliest followers of Jesus that "their experience of Jesus still calling on them to continue his message and life style was the substance of their resurrection experience."[46]

All three gospels spell it out with a parable, the familiar parable of the man who entrusts money into the keeping of his slaves. Each deals with it differently and suffers a different fate. The teachings of Jesus have been entrusted to us, and what we do with them will determine our spiritual fate. The irony here is that this understanding really fits Thomas better than it fits Matthew or Luke.[47]

The last promise Jesus makes in Q is rather puzzling.

You who have followed me, will sit on thrones judging the twelve tribes of Israel.[48]

One scholar, James Tabor, has developed a theory that Jesus really did have a political outcome in mind, in which each of the twelve disciples would have a political kingdom of his own where the teachings of Jesus could be enforced.[49] However, if my reading of the "Sayings Gospel Q" is in any measure correct, it would be highly unlikely that he would believe the internal nature of the Kingdom and the ways of compassion, love, and peace could be enhanced by political enforcement. If the Q document should turn out to be nothing more than an hypothesis, Tabor's theory, based on the discovery of what has been called the "Jesus family tomb," might turn out to be more accurate than it now appears to be. Corroboration of Tabor's theory will have to wait.

Scholars like James Robinson believe that its sayings are the closest we can ever get to what Jesus actually said, though its source was an oral tradition that had evolved during the first decades after Jesus' death, with all the disadvantages that word of mouth entails.

White sums up the general scholarly evaluation: "Apart from Paul, it is the earliest discoverable layer of the Jesus tradition. Nonetheless, it reflects a secondary stage of transmission since its preserved form comes from a stage of composition in Greek."[50]

Robinson also admits this oldest layer is not necessarily reliable, but it is the best we can do. He warns, "Otherwise Jesus quite unnecessarily disappears from the pages of history, or 'Jesus' becomes an empty category into which wild fantasies can be poured."[51]

The Writing of the New Testament Gospels

Mark was written for Gentile readers very early in the 70s CE, Matthew a little later in the 70s. Luke-Acts, a two volume work by a Gentile author writing for Gentiles, was probably written in the 80s CE. It is clear that Q was already in existence when Matthew and Luke were written because both are a blending of Mark and Q. Matthew appears to have been written for a Jewish Christian audience, as was the Q document. John wasn't written until the 90s CE or even later.

Luke clearly devalues the early Jewish Christian tradition, and in his "Acts of the Apostles" all but ignores its existence.[52] He begins his history of the church with Paul's ministry in the 50s CE. Since Acts is the only church history to be included in the New Testament canon, most Christians today are unfortunately unaware of the early Jesus movement. The search for self-identity of the Gentile Christian portion of the movement took another step forward with the writing of Luke-Acts.

Evidence of this is that, following the temptation story, Satan is said by Luke to have given up. There follows, then, his material from Q. After citing Q sources, Luke returns to Mark for the rest of Jesus' public ministry in his passion and death.

That is, Luke is treating the teaching ministry of Jesus as applying only to an ideal world in which Satan is not active. But when Satan becomes active again, new instructions are necessary; for example, instead of no sword, two swords will be sufficient.[53] Thus, it seems clear that Luke is a part of the self-identification process which the Gentile branch of the Jesus movement underwent. That process involved the shifting of the emphasis away from Jesus' own countercultural teachings and the treatment of the righteousness of Jesus as a perfect obedience to the old law.[54]

However, Paul does speak of faith acting through love as the appropriate way for the followers of Jesus to behave in the new age of the Spirit. But there is strong reason to believe that the teachings of the historical Jesus found in Q were themselves understood by Q to be the conduct "fit for repentance." They were God reigning, or signs of the Kingdom already arriving.

Robinson also admits that "the Gospel of Luke does present Jesus' public ministry in Galilee and then the first chapters of Acts do describe the Jerusalem church, but just in order to have them validate Paul's Gentile church."[55]

Acts itself is written as though the teachings of Q, and the Q community of Jewish Christians, no longer existed. This fact lends weight to the belief that there had existed a Q community which had been a part of the early history of the Jesus movement. In fact, the references in the Q document to the rejection of the disciples and to the wisdom of children, as opposed to the stubbornness of the adults, suggest that the Q message may have already been in trouble when it was written down. It was a message that simply did not sound realistic to sophisticated persons. Nevertheless, it is reasonable to believe that the Q community of Jewish Christians closest to Jesus himself was the earliest form of the Jesus movement contending for dominance. But gradually, it disappeared with only Matthew, Luke, and the Gnostic *Gospel of Thomas* preserving the hypothetical "Sayings Gospel Q."

The Gospel of John, written somewhere between 90 and 120 CE, represents an even greater degree of separation from Judaism and rejection of the early Jesus movement. It is more valuable for its theological content than its history and reflects the increasing impact of Greek thought on the life of the evolving Christian community.

The church that emerged out of this contentious amalgam is still very much the church of today.

Mention should be made here of the group of scholars known as the "The Jesus Seminar." This group came on the scene twenty or more years ago and initiated its own search for the historical Jesus. A number of popular books have been published by some of the members of the group, and I want to refer to one of those books. It is *Jesus, A Revolutionary Biography,* by John Dominic Crossan, a Roman Catholic scholar. He sees Epictetus, a Greek cynic, as the best interpreter of Jesus. Epictetus' knowledge of the historical Jesus could have been, at best, no better than our own since he lived from around 60 CE to around 130 CE and Jesus was a Jewish peasant who had died at least thirty years before Epictetus was born. This is another case of reinterpretation in terms of Greek/Roman thought and it has enabled Crossan to "reconstruct" Jesus.[56]

Such reconstructions from questionable sources, such as the canonical gospels, speculations based on a knowledge of the culture and history of Jesus' times, plus the importation of Gentile concepts far removed from those of the Jewish world view, usually disregard the requirements of historical dependability. In fact, the use of non-Jewish categories of thought is precisely what enabled the sect to become a cult and the Jesus movement to become a church.

So the question remains: what can we reasonably believe about Jesus?

Chapter 3

✦

What We Can Know and Can't

Christianity[57] is always characterized as a historical religion, along with Judaism and Islam, while such religions as Taoism, Scientology, Hinduism, and Spiritualism do not claim to be based on historical events. The focal historical event of the Christian religion is the birth, life, and death of Jesus of Nazareth. But this is an almost scandalous claim when the fact is we know very little about the historical events on which the Christian faith is based.

It would, of course, be a disaster for the Christian world if it turned out, as some atheists are still claiming, that there never was such a person as Jesus of Nazareth. To be sure, they are right when they remind us that the four Gospels are totally based on oral traditions that evolved during a period of forty years and more following his death.[58] I share with them their skepticism about our knowledge concerning the historical figure of Jesus. However, their extreme reaction probably represents a naive, wholesale rejection of the history of the early church and its politically oriented establishment, with its sacred literature and its dogmas thrown in, rather than attention to the historical evidence that, in fact, does exist for Jesus' birth and death.

To put it bluntly, it is not necessary to reject the historical existence of Jesus in order to seriously question orthodox teachings about Jesus, or even to doubt many of the events and sayings of Jesus which the canonical gospels report. That said, we do know a few things with as much certainty as we know any historical event.

The Criteria for Historicity

It will be helpful at this point to know how it is possible to determine what things are historically certain, what are probable, what are possible but unlikely, and those that are certainly not true. The following is a summation of the criteria as set forth by Bart Ehrman:

First, historians look for certain kinds of evidence.

1. They look for numerous sources of evidence for the same event.
2. They look for evidence that comes from a point in time as close as possible to the event.
3. They look for evidence that is independent of other evidence.
4. They look for evidence that does not contradict other evidence.
5. They look for evidence that is internally consistent.
6. They look for no biases.

Second, they apply the following criteria in order to make judgments about the events in question.

• Independent Attestation

Biblical sources may be independent when it is clear the authors are different. For instance, that Jesus had brothers is attested to by Mark, Paul, and Josephus. However, it doesn't work when the evidence from one source conflicts with that from another because it doesn't tell us which one is false. Additionally, other criteria may indicate that none is true.

• Dissimilarity

When a claim casts a negative light on Jesus, it is more likely to be true because the writer is interested in casting the most positive light possible on Jesus and would not likely report an unfavorable fact unless it were undeniably true. For example, the baptism of Jesus by John seems to show John's superiority to Jesus. Matthew even has Jesus protesting that John should not baptize him. One must always consider the vested interest of the author.

• Contextual Credibility

This criterion implies, among other things, that the closer the evidence is to Jesus himself, the more likely it is to be true, but the variety of social and theological contexts from which the evidence comes is equally important. Nicodemus, whose story appears only in the Gospel of John, is reported to have misunderstood Jesus' reference to "born again a second time." The Greek in which this story is recounted has two meanings for the expression, while Aramaic, in which the event would have taken place, does not. Nicodemus would not have misunderstood since there would have been only one way to understand the expression. So the story, as told, does not make sense. It was common for Christians to make up stories to fit their theological purposes. This happened with both orthodox Christians and with Gnostic Christians. Even Jewish and Muslim sources claim to report sayings of Jesus, but their stories are probably biased, so even if true, they cannot be trusted. This criterion can establish probability, but not certainty. All three criteria must be used together.[59]

Jesus Was a Jewish Man

The first and most obvious thing we know with certainty about Jesus is that he was a real, historical Jewish man. We know with equal certainty that he was executed by the Romans somewhere between 26 and 29 CE. We know this with the greatest certainty because independent sources tell us. The most certain of these sources is that of the Roman historian Tacitus who, in 117 CE following his account of the great fire in Rome in 64 CE, wrote as follows:

> *Nero fastened the guilt and inflicted the most exquisite tortures on a class hated for their abominations, called Christians by the populace. Christus, from whom the name had its origin, suffered the extreme penalty during the reign of Tiberias, at the hands of one of his procurators, Pontius Pilate, and a most mischievous superstition thus checked for the moment, again broke out, not only in Judea, the first source of the evil, but even in Rome where all things hideous and shameful from every part of the world find their center and become popular.[60]*

This obviously hostile account is the surest historical testimony to Jesus' existence and his death, but it leaves the rest of the story in darkness.

The other independent source for the historicity of Jesus comes from the Jewish general and historian, Josephus. It reads, in part, "About this time came Jesus, a wise man. For he was a performer of paradoxical feats, a teacher of the people who accept the unusual with pleasure, and he won over many of the Jews and also many Greeks. And the tribe of the Christians, so named after him, has not disappeared to this day."[61]

From these two external sources, we obviously know he was born, had a following, and died during Pilate's administration, probably between 26 and 29 CE. They do not, however, give any indication of the date of his birth.

The Gregorian calendar, by which most cultures on the earth live, also does not give us an exact date for Jesus' birth. However, scholars have determined that he was born somewhere between 7 and 4 BCE. It had to have been by 4 BCE because Herod's rule ended in that year.

Matthew and Luke say it happened in Bethlehem, but Mark simply says he came from Nazareth. Likely, he was born in Nazareth because both Matthew and Luke, written more than seventy years later, were interested in finding a way to connect him to the house of David from whence the Messiah, according to Hebrew prophecy, was to come. So Luke tells the story of a census that required Joseph and Mary to go to Bethlehem, the city of David, to be registered. However, the first census, taken under Quirinius, didn't take place until 6 CE, at least ten years after Herod had died.

The accounts in these two gospels were colored by the perspective of writers needing to certify the Messiahship of Jesus for their readers—Matthew for his Jewish readers and Luke for his Gentile readers. So the story of Joseph and Mary's journey to Bethlehem, the city of David, is highly suspect. We really don't know.

We do, however, know quite a bit about the world in which Jesus was born, lived, and died. Therefore, we can assume certain things about his views and his experiences as a young man. Beyond that, we don't know very much. For example, it is almost certain that Jesus spoke Aramaic. He is also reported to have read from the Hebrew scriptures, but that report has him reading from two widely separate parts of Isaiah's prophecy, which would have been extremely difficult to do from a traditional scroll. Most laypersons in those days did not know Hebrew at all and were illiterate as well, so we don't really know if Jesus knew Hebrew or not.

Jesus may have known some Greek since recent archeological excavations have revealed that Nazareth was about four miles from the Greek-speaking city of Sepphoris. In fact, Joseph may well have been involved in the construction of that city since it occurred during Jesus' lifetime. No doubt Jesus himself was familiar with the city and, perhaps, with the language. But that is only a speculation.

Because of so many sources, it is highly probable that Jesus' parents were Joseph and Mary. Mark, Paul, and Josephus all say that he had brothers—among them James, who later led the Jesus movement in Jerusalem.

Jesus' connection with John the Baptist is also reasonably certain. All the gospels report it. Josephus does as well; he provides a curious twist on the relationship, however. He suggests that Jesus was a follower of John and that he struck out on his own ministry only after John had been murdered. James Tabor also discusses this relationship at length and speculates concerning the shift in focus that Jesus brought to his ministry after John's death. He concludes that Jesus set out to establish what he calls a "dynasty" led by the twelve disciples.[62] Who really knows?

We are also not sure how long Jesus' ministry lasted. The Gospel of John describes three different Passover seasons, while the other gospels mention only one. Therefore, the tradition of a three-year ministry comes from John. Otherwise, it would appear that his ministry lasted less than a year. Mark certainly gives that impression. But then his account is spare and hurried, and he may well have ignored a couple of Passovers. So, again, we do not know.

What about the miracles Jesus is reported to have performed? The most we know is that it was an age when magic and miracles were widely reported. In fact, Josephus and Tacitus both report that he had a reputation for performing miracles, "paradoxical feats," and healings. Such occurrences were not doubted until the Age of Enlightenment began to raise questions.

We know some of the sayings which, during the course of a brief ministry, he is remembered to have uttered, but the accuracy of those sayings is somewhat shaky. The teachings of Jesus reported in the four Gospels of the New Testament have probably received more scholarly attention than any other aspect of the canonical gospels. Some of his apocalyptic sayings seem incompatible with other teachings about peacemaking and compassion.

We've already looked at the theories that have been constructed concerning the relationships among the first three gospels and the

Gospel of Thomas. The Gospel of John seems unrelated to the others because of his different theology and major differences in chronology. John also does not repeat any of the sayings from the other three accounts. However, most scholars recognize what James Robinson calls the "Sayings Gospel Q" as providing a major piece of the relationship linking the other gospels.

All four canonical gospels and Tacitus agree that Jesus died on a Roman cross in Jerusalem under Pontius Pilate, who ruled from 26 to 36 CE according to Roman sources. If, as Luke says, Jesus began his ministry at thirty years of age, then 4 BCE plus thirty years is 26 CE, and his death would have occurred one to three years later. However, they differ on the immediate cause of his execution. Mark says it was because of the cleansing of the Temple, but John has the cleansing of the Temple occurring at the beginning of Jesus' ministry. Matthew seems to blame the triumphal entry for the execution, thus suggesting a political cause. Later came the claim that God was responsible, but that was a judgment made from a certain theological perspective, not an historical conclusion. The exact date of Jesus' crucifixion is uncertain.

As to the resurrection, all four canonical gospels report that he rose on the third day following his execution. Matthew alone reports guards around the tomb. Mark and Matthew have Jesus appearing to his disciples only in Galilee, and Luke only in Jerusalem and the vicinity, while John records appearances in both locations. Luke alone reports a forty-day sojourn on earth before Jesus' ascension into heaven.[63] We know that reports of resurrection of the gods were common in that day. Recently, some evidence has also been discovered that suggests a tradition existed that the Messiah would be resurrected on the third day. The gospel writers often used prophecies and ancient traditions to bolster their narrative claims, but there is no historical evidence for the bodily resurrection of Jesus.

Beyond these partial and tentative suggestions, we can be sure of almost nothing. The problem is that how one sees Jesus depends on one's perspective. Those who really knew the historical Jesus were his closest friends and a few other people in Galilee and Jerusalem, but neither they, nor Jesus himself, appear to have written anything down. In fact, most of them were probably illiterate.

What are we to do with the facts we have then? And how should we treat the probabilities? There is even the question as to what to do with those stories that are part of the tradition, but which have no basis whatsoever in historically known fact.

The easy and totally irresponsible answer often given to these questions is that of the inerrancy of holy scripture. That is, God inspired certain persons to write down the facts according to his perfect knowledge. Therefore, all these questions are irrelevant, if not also irreverent.

However, most "strict constructionists" (read "fundamentalists") are ready to admit that through the centuries since the New Testament gospels were first written down under God's inspiration, they inevitably underwent calculated editing and suffered errors in the process of hand-copying which had preserved them prior to Gutenberg's invention of movable type. Thus, they are now in a corrupted state. But, they affirm that the original copies, which no longer exist, were, in fact, a perfect representation of that which God inspired the original authors to write down. Now, that is at least a somewhat more responsible explanation for the discrepancies and errors.

But the premise is completely incapable of historical support. That is, we have no way of comparing the nonexistent originals with what we now possess in our modern Bibles. Unable to consult the originals, we are left with no certain knowledge at all, and the doctrine of verbal inspiration becomes useless.

That is why we must employ the tools of scholars if the Bible is to be anything more than an artifact for museum shelves.

As I have already indicated, however, Q has given us a tentative idea about some of the teachings of the enigmatical figure of Jesus of Nazareth.

Jesus the Teacher

The theme of the Kingdom of God goes back, of course, to the prophecies of Isaiah and Jeremiah. But the hope of God's intervention arose in the latter half of the third century BCE. However, many Jews became weary of waiting and early in the second century BCE decided to take things into their own hands. Led by the Maccabees, they revolted against successive oppressors and were always brutally squelched. From there on, it was often difficult to separate the revolutionary passion from the hope for God's intervention. In this context, Jesus apparently talked about the Kingdom of God.

This means we must now make a much closer examination of the content of the "Sayings Gospel Q," but we must be careful about making too strong a claim for it. According to scholars, the hypothesis that the Q gospel once existed is probably true, but the sayings found in Q do not have a secure standing as historical, at least according to the criteria of historicity that we have already discussed. Did Jesus actually teach these things? It seems likely. Certainly it is the closest we can come.

Of course, Jesus said many other things as well. Some of the sayings discussed below may well have been inaccurately reported to begin with. The Q Gospel itself may have been edited and modified more than once by the time it reached the hands of Mathew and Luke, but there is continuity present in the document as reconstructed.

When Constantine, many years later, called the Council of Nicea, the decision it reached was to affirm a hellenized, or Greek-influenced, version of the message that Paul had preached. The teachings of Jesus were no longer the Gospel, meaning the good news, but the theological teaching about who Jesus was assumed that role.

It was Francis of Assissi and his followers who first reclaimed the teachings of Jesus, insofar as they were available in his time. Leo Tolstoy renewed them in *War and Peace*. Then came Mahatma Gandhi and Martin Luther King Jr., and all modeled the message of Q in their own way.[64]

In any case, this is the best we have been able to do in our effort to understand more about the teachings of Jesus, the Jewish man who probably walked throughout Israel and Judea teaching the people about the Kingdom of God. It is also almost certain that these teachings constitute the gospel to which the Roman soldiers were first converted, and that preceded even Paul's version of the gospel.

Assuming that Q was once a written document, though no copy has ever been found, it is still known through its appearance in Matthew, Luke, and *Thomas*. What is known as the "Sermon on the Mount" in Luke, or as the "Sermon on the Plain" in Matthew, is the heart of Q. Robinson calls it "the Gospel of Jesus."

Robinson has also provided the translation from the Greek from which I am quoting in the following examination of the Q message, so it will differ a bit from the translations that you will find in Matthew and Luke in your own New Testament.

In the following description of the content of Q, I shall mix occasional quotations with a summary of the message and observations of my own. The observations are intended both to interpret meanings and to reveal the coherence of the whole.

The order of the material, as it appears in Luke, is judged to follow that of Q more closely than Matthew does. This is due to the fact that Luke wasn't much interested in the teaching part of the story and was eager to get on to the passion story which underwrote Paul's interpretation of the gospel. Luke was also more interested, in the Acts of the Apostles, in telling the story of the Gentile church which was already in the process of separating itself from Judaism. However, Matthew was much more inclined to weave the sayings of Jesus into the narrative because, for his Jewish readers, the teachings were still highly important.

Here then is the gist of Q as Robinson and his team of scholars have deciphered it after many years of work.

The Setting

The "Sayings Gospel Q" begins with a short description of John's ministry in the region of the Jordan River. John then announces the coming of the Kingdom about which I have already commented.

He said to the crowds coming to be baptized: Snakes' litter, who warned you to run from the impending rage? So bear fruit worthy of repentance, and do not presume to tell yourselves. We have a forefather Abraham! For I tell you: God can produce children for Abraham right out of these rocks! And the ax already lies at the root of the trees. So every tree not bearing healthy fruit is to be chopped down and thrown into the fire.

—Luke 3:7–9 and Matthew 3:7–10

Thus, we are warned immediately that Jesus' version of the apocalypse is going to be different. A new order of conduct is to be required of the "children of Abraham." Their heredity, however, has nothing to do with it. Furthermore, the nature of the coming Kingdom is quite different from some cataclysmic event perpetrated by God's intervention, which had been the Jewish apocalyptic for over two hundred years. The teachings of Jesus in Q suggest that the miracles and healings of Jesus are God already reigning, and that the "fruits worthy of repentance" will be the people's participation in the reigning of God, the coming of the Kingdom.

Then John predicts the coming of the "one who is to come after me," the one who will baptize with the "Spirit and fire" (Luke 3:16b–17 and Matthew 3:11–12).

John baptizes Jesus (Luke 3:21b–22 and Matthew 316–17), who then goes into the wilderness where he is unsuccessfully tempted by Satan, and then Satan leaves him (Luke 4:1–12 and Matthew 4:1–11).

The Beatitudes

The scene now moves back to Nazareth, and then quickly on to what has come to be called the "Sermon on the Mount," which is built around the Beatitudes. Here we hear the essential Jesus speaking, at least as near as we will ever come to actually hearing him. The first beatitude blesses "the poor." The original literally referred to the poor in worldly goods, which was the condition of the earliest Jesus followers. Their condition was formalized in their name, the Ebionites, a name meaning "the poor" in Aramaic. Blessings on the hungry, the mourners, and the persecuted follow (Luke 6:20–23; Matthew 5:1–4, 11–12; and Thomas 54:69). Each beatitude is a promise of "God reigning." Therefore, the original apocalyptic message of Jesus, if it is actually reflected in Q, had taken quite a different tack from Paul's teaching about the coming Kingdom. But this was the original Kingdom promise. This was the good news Jesus brought.

Now for the "fruits worthy of repentance." Jesus talks about loving your enemies, and how the rain falls on the just and the unjust (Luke 6:27–28, 35c–d; and Matthew 5:44–45). The message of God reigning, as it applies to the just and the unjust, is also a message of God's unconditional love or grace. So the Kingdom is already coming, and all are urged to participate in its coming. Everyone, in other words, has a part in the coming Kingdom, and God continues to reign through them. No longer is the Kingdom seen to be a violent event in which a powerful, independent, theistic God intervenes to overthrow the political powers that threaten Israel's existence.

Not only must we love our enemies as God loves even the unjust, but we must also be willing to renounce our own rights, or turn the other cheek, and go the second mile (Luke 6:29–30, Matthew 5:39b–42, and Thomas 95). There follows the Golden Rule, of which there are other versions from other sources as well (Luke 6:31, Matthew 7:12, and Thomas 6:3). The classic description of the love with which his followers are to treat others is stated as follows:

> *If you love those who love you, what credit is that to you? For even sinners love those who love them. ... If you lend to those from whom you hope to receive, what credit is that to you? Even sinners lend to sinners to receive as much again. (Luke 6:32, 34, Matthew 5:46–47, and Thomas 95)*

Jesus contrasts unconditional love with the loveless practices of the tax collectors or, according to Matthew's version, the Gentiles. He calls for pity like God's pity (Luke 6:32, 34, 36; Matthew 5:46–48; and Thomas 95). He states that judging others is very unwise because you become subject to the same judgment—an attack on hypocrisy.

Jesus' Followers as Teachers

There is now a transition to the responsibilities of those who would teach others the fruits of repentance. The blind cannot lead the blind (Luke 6:39, Matthew 15:14, and Thomas 34) and the responsibility of the learner is to imitate his teacher, not just listen to him. This, therefore, requires integrity on the part of the teacher (Luke 6:40 and Matthew 10:24–25a). Hypocrisy does not befit the teacher and piety cannot take the place of integrity (Luke 6:41–42, 6:46; and Matthew 7:3–5, 7:21).

The "Sermon on the Mount" ends with Jesus' words reinforcing the importance of his teachings—because only by building your life upon them as its foundation can you share in God's reigning (Luke 6:47–49 and Matthew 7:24–27). This is, of course, the familiar passage about building one's house on a rock rather than upon shifting sand. Here Jesus is attributing salvation to the observance of his teachings about grace, or unconditional love, rather than faith in the power of his death to assure the availability of God's grace. God's grace is already in action.

The Q document continues then with a certain amount of narration. A centurion trusts Jesus' teachings, and John and Jesus hold a conversation. When John asks if Jesus is the one to come, Jesus simply points out the healing he is doing as a sign of God's reigning. At the same time, he warns his own followers about the difficulty of following his own teachings, because one will always be criticized, no matter what one does. Referring to John, he says, "Yet the least significant in God's kingdom is more than he" (Luke 7:31–35 and Matthew 11:16–19).

Someone then approaches Jesus about becoming his follower. Jesus warns him that he may have nowhere to lay his head, and that he will have to abandon the ordinary custom of burying his dead father. This will, of course, make him an outsider in the community (Luke 9:57–60, Matthew 8:19–22, and Thomas 86).

Now we learn that Jesus is in need of help to spread his teachings. This issue is discussed in a more or less ordered fashion in Luke 10:2–16, and in a more scattered manner in Matthew 9:37–38, 10:7–16, 40, 11:21–24. These are warnings about what problems his followers can expect to meet when they go from town to town, and suggestions on how to deal with them.

At this point, Jesus' prayer reflects his frustration with the sophisticates who cannot hear him or accept his countercultural message.

He said: I praise you Father, Lord of heaven and earth, for you hid these things from sages and the learned, and disclosed them to children. Yes, Father, for that is what it has pleased you to do.

—Luke 10:21 and Matthew 11:25–26

The suggestion of the father and son relationship here may suggest a source for the later doctrine of the Trinity. But here it cannot have that implication, for Jesus is simply talking about the truth of his teachings, which he believes God has revealed to him. That is, his relation to God is like that of a son who is taught by his father. This passage appears also in Thomas, which nowhere suggests that Jesus was anything other than an inspired human teacher. Though Thomas may have assumed a Docetic view of Jesus, he does not imply that Jesus was anything other than what his disciples were expected also to become.

Jesus continues:

Blessed are the eyes that see what you see. For I tell you: Many prophets and kings wanted to see what you see, but never saw it and to hear what you hear, but never heard it.

—Luke 10:23b–24, Matthew 13:16–17

Finally, this section of Q concludes with what has come to be known as the Lord's Prayer and Jesus' teaching about prayer.

So if you, though evil, know how to give good gifts to your children, by how much more will the Father from heaven give good things to those who ask him!

—Luke 11:9–13, Matthew, 7:7–11, and Thomas 92:1, 9

Again, the answers to prayer are manifestations of God reigning— of the presence of the Kingdom which is in the process of coming.

An Exorcism

At this point, we come to the report of an exorcism in which Jesus defends himself against the accusation that he has acted by the power of Beelzebub rather than God (Luke 11:14–15, 17–26, and Matthew 9:32–34, 12:25–30, 43–45).

He uses an analogy for God's power to cast out demons.

A strong person's house cannot be looted, but if someone still stronger over powers him, he does get looted.

—Luke 11:21–22 and Matthew 12:9

A demon can resist the lesser power of Beelzebub, but it takes the greater power of God to cast out a strong demon. Such an exorcism is another manifestation of God's reigning in Jesus' announcement of the coming Kingdom.

A saying related to the exorcism follows.

The one not with me is against me, and the one not gathering with me scatters.

—Luke 11:23 and Matthew 12:30

But Jesus immediately goes on to warn them that evil spirits are likely to return, multiplied in strength. Vigilance is always necessary (Luke 11:24–26 and Matthew 12:43–45). An admonition about hearing and keeping God's instructions follows.

Jesus' response to some of his hearers' demands for a sign is to compare himself to Jonah. In other words, he himself is the only sign they will be given because he embodies his own teachings in his lifestyle. He does what he teaches (Luke 11:16, 29–33, and Matthew 2:38–43).

The final Q reference to Jesus' teaching ministry is a kind of justification for his message.

No one lights a lamp and sets it in a hidden place but on the lamp stand and it gives light for everyone in the house.

—Luke 11:33, Matthew 5:15, and Thomas 33:2–3

Hypocrisy

Now Jesus begins his attack on the Pharisees, who have totally distorted the duties of a "good" Jew. He sees his own teachings as in direct opposition to the teaching practice of the Pharisees, and he views them as hypocrites. This is Jesus' intent when he talks about the eyes as the lamp of the body (Luke 11:34–35 and Matthew 6:22–23), and how they clean the outside of the cup and leave the inside impure (Luke 11:42, 39b, 41–44; Matthew 23:6-7, 23, 25, 26b–27) and Thomas 89). Jesus explains that their hypocrisy has to do with the formalities of religious practice and the Pharisees' flaunting of their own importance.

And woe to you, exegetes of the Law, for you bind ... burdens and loads on the backs of people, but you yourselves do not want to lift a finger to move them.

—Luke 11:46b, Matthew 23:4, and Thomas 39:1–2

An accounting will be required of those who have killed the prophets and sages (Luke 11:49–51 and Matthew 23:34–36). Jesus further warns that the guilty will be exposed (Luke 12:2–3. Matthew 10:26–27, and Thomas 5:2).

Assurance

Having put the Pharisees in their place, Jesus assures his followers that they need not fear those who can kill the body, but not the soul. Clearly Jesus and his followers were in harm's way when they challenged the values and standards of the establishment. "You are more precious to God," Jesus told them, "than many sparrows, and you will not fall unless God permits it." Also, he states that he will be the advocate before the angels for those who speak out for him. Clearly he is seeing that his life and the lives of his followers are at risk.

However, Jesus seems now to want to clarify just what he is saying. He explains that those who speak against his person will be forgiven, but those who speak against the Holy Spirit, who has given him the teachings he propounds, will not be forgiven (Luke 12:4–10 and Matthew 10:8, 29–33). More important even than the teacher are the teachings, because the teachings have been inspired by the Spirit. This would seem to be a definitive rejection, by Jesus, of Paul's later focus on who Jesus was, rather than on what Jesus taught. The doctrines affirming Jesus to be uniquely divine and of the same substance as the Father would have been roundly rejected by Jesus had he caught wind of them. As would the claim that salvation was to be attained by faith in the atonement effected by Jesus' death on the cross.

What to Do Now

Jesus feels it necessary to counsel his listeners about what to do when they are charged. First, don't worry about what to say if you are brought before the Sanhedrin, because the Spirit will tell you. Neither should you worry about your future welfare, for God will see to it even as he takes care of the ravens. Only the Gentiles worry about these things, but good Jews do not.

Seek first his Kingdom and all these shall be granted to you.

—Luke 12:31, Matthew 6:33, and Thomas 36:1

Be Prepared

Jesus tells them to be ready, for this Kingdom will come like a thief in the night. Or, when a master entrusts his goods to his servant while he is gone, the servant must always be ready for he does not know when the master will return (Luke 12:39–40; Matthew 24:43–44; and Thomas 21:5, 103). The teachings have been entrusted to them and must be kept against the day of accounting. This is their stewardship.

Jesus then reverts to his earlier apocalyptic predictions for he talks about "fire on the earth," and how families will be divided. It will not be a time of peace, but of great struggle and suffering. There is no indication that it will be a time of armed conflict or the overthrow of Rome, but he seems to believe the confrontation between his teachings and the teachings of the rabbis and the Gentiles will eventually reach a tipping point. Why should he not think that?

Anyway, you cannot predict when such a conflict will take place in the same way that you predict the weather by certain signs (Luke 12:54–56, Matthew 10:34–35, and Thomas 16:1–2).

If legal actions are brought, you should try to settle your differences out of court because the court may not be able to understand your case. The implication may be that the court will likely side with the established wisdom (Luke 12:58–59 and Matthew 5:25–26).

What Is the Kingdom Like?

The Kingdom is like a tiny mustard seed because it is made up of the smallest things—the little signs of God reigning, like turning the other cheek and all the other things that Jesus has been teaching them (Luke 13:18–19, Matthew 13:31–32, and Thomas).

The Kingdom is also like yeast—it is often not noticed, but it is always working (Luke 13:20–21, Matthew 13:33, and Thomas).

Who Gets In?

It's not easy to enter the Kingdom, Jesus says. It will do one no good to claim entrance by virtue of having been associated with him at some time in the past. Rather, one must do the things he teaches (Luke 13:24–27 and Matthew 7:13–14, 22–23; 25:10–12). In fact, many will be part of the Kingdom of God reigning, who come from afar, and whom you would never expect to see there (Luke 13:29 and Matthew 8:11). Ordinary standards of preference will not qualify anyone for participation in the Kingdom (Luke 13:30, Matthew 20:16, and Thomas 4:2).

Jesus says he weeps for all those whom he loves, and whom he longs to see in the Kingdom but who are unwilling. Their only hope will be to see him on the day when they say, "Blessed is the one who comes in the name of the Lord." That is, when they believe what he has taught and do it. That, after all, is what it means to have a Lord (Luke 13:34–35 and Matthew 23:37–39). Those who think they are worthy to come into the Kingdom will be disappointed, but those who do not expect to make it will be welcomed, for they will have followed his teachings (Luke 14:11 and Matthew 23:12).

Then, Jesus tells a parable about a large dinner to whom many were invited, but to which few came because so many had an excuse—other things had priority (Luke 14:16–18, 19, 21, 23; Matthew 22:2–3, 5, 7a, 8–10; and Thomas). Those who do not give the teachings of the Kingdom priority cannot come. Not even members of their families can have priority over the teachings of the Kingdom (Luke 14:26, Matthew 10:37, and Thomas 64).

Jesus then speaks of taking up his cross. In the context of the Q document, the cross can only mean the willingness to face the consequences of participating in the actions of God reigning (Luke 14:27, Matthew 10:38, and Thomas 55:2). "The one who finds one's life will lose it, and the one who loses one's life for my sake will find it" (Luke 17:33 and Matthew 10:39). Again we see where, for Jesus, the priority must lie. One must face the consequences of following the teachings of Jesus.

The reigning of God is like salt, he suggests. It makes a difference. If it makes no difference, it is useless (Luke 14:34–35 and Matthew 5:13). You see, you must make a choice. You can't have it both ways. Either you follow the usual way of leading your life, or you choose to participate in God's reigning as Jesus has taught and is doing (Luke 16:13, Matthew 6:24, and Thomas 47:2).

Everything has changed since John came, says Jesus. Before, we had the words of the prophets and the rules of the law. They served the Kingdom well, but now they are violated as John has said. But the Law remains and will remain (Luke 16:16–17 and Matthew 5:18, 11:12–13). Clearly Jesus was not putting down the old law, but rather the hypocrisies practiced by the leadership of the current established religion. Apparently, he himself had never adopted the attitude toward the law that Paul would later espouse. Nevertheless, it was his teaching that constituted the "fruit worthy of repentance," and that took priority for him.

We would surely like to ask him about some of these things, wouldn't we?

Assorted Teachings

Everyone who divorces his wife and marries another, commits adultery, and the one who marries a divorcee commits adultery.

—Luke 16:18 and Matthew 5:32

There follows a warning against those who tempt a child (Luke 17:1–2 and Matthew 18:6, 7).

There is also the story of the single sheep that was lost, and how the shepherd rejoices when he finds it. Every single person who returns to the way of the Kingdom after straying will cause great rejoicing. Similarly, the lost coin occasions an eager search (Luke 15:4–5a, 7–10; Matthew 18:12–13 [though the coin story is missing from Matthew]; and Thomas 107). There is always hope for the wayward sheep or the lost coin because, along the way of the Kingdom, one is called to forgive endlessly (Luke 17:3 and Matthew 18:15–21).

Now the mustard seed comes in for recognition again. This time Jesus compares effective faith with the tiniest mustard seed. In other words, faith begins very small, but it grows until it can do great things (Luke 17:6, Matthew17:20b, and Thomas 48).

The nature of the Kingdom becomes clearer yet. It is not, Jesus says, something God sends from outside. Rather, the way of the Kingdom is a way of life which arises from within (Luke 17:20–21; Matthew 24:23; and Thomas 3:1–3, 113). So, will you see Jesus, this "son of humanity," when he comes? Apparently not as his listeners are accustomed to thinking of it. They thought of it as the salvation of Israel from oppression. But his way will cover the whole earth (Luke

17:23–24, Matthew 24:26–27, and Thomas 3:1–2). Here it becomes clear why the Jesus people were first called the people of "the Way."

Wherever the corpse; there the vultures will gather.

—Luke 17:37 and Matthew 24:28

Perhaps Jesus is suggesting that those who do not enter upon the way of the Kingdom will die and disappear.

Similarly, on the day of reckoning, the people will be like those who were going about the affairs of their everyday life, paying no attention to the ways of the Kingdom. Then Noah comes with the ark, but the flood sweeps all the careless people away (Luke 17:26–27, 30; and Matthew 24:37–39).

Then Jesus says,

I tell you: There will be two men in the field; one is taken and one is left. Two women will be grinding at the mill; one is taken and one is left.

—Luke 17:34, 35; Matthew 24:40–41; and Thomas 61:1

There is simply no other way to tell who will be saved and who will not. It all depends on who has followed the teachings.

Now comes the parable of the master who entrusts his money to his slaves while he goes on a trip. Each slave treats the money differently and is rewarded differently. The investment of what has been entrusted to you is what is required. It probably refers to one's stewardship of the teachings one has heard. Does one ignore them or follow them? But it may have a broader application, for the parable closes with the following:

For to everyone who has will be given; but from the one who does not have, even what he has will be taken from him.

—Luke 19:12–13, 15:24, 26; Matthew 25:14–15b, 19–29; and Thomas 41

Finally, the puzzler. "You who have followed me will sit on thrones judging the twelve tribes of Israel (Luke 22:28 and Matthew 19:28)

Quite amazing is the fact that the realized eschatology found in these teachings of Jesus appears to prefigure, in a striking manner, the realized eschatology of the Gnostic literature as it is reflected in the *Gospel of Thomas*. The Kingdom of God is seen to be constituted of the merciful and grace-filled acts of God, that is, of God reigning, rather than some kind of perfect, kingly realm. Therefore, the countercultural teachings of Jesus, which were intended to show his followers how to participate in God's reigning, may also have been precipitating factors in his murder.

When he invites his followers to bear the cross, he is inviting them to take the risk of being crucified as he was. That is to say, the "day of wrath" refers to the violence that will surely be perpetrated by the enemies of the Way. But the Kingdom itself is coming already in every deed of grace profound. Thus Jesus' own way of salvation stands in stark contrast to Paul's and the theologically orthodox treatment of Jesus' death as atonement. Moreover, it is clear his view of the apocalypse had already anticipated the need for its revision long before the destruction of the Temple forced it. Once again, we see how the orthodoxy of the later church was, in fact, an intrusion into the life of the Jesus movement.

Of course, the teachings of Jesus we find in the "Sayings Gospel Q" have been identified simply through the use of a scholarly theory. How that came about is imaginatively suggested by Andrew Philip Smith, in *The Lost Sayings of Jesus*: "The sayings of Jesus are like a river flowing down from its mountain source. As the river gathers momentum, tributaries join it and become a part of the river, swelling its flow. Before the river reaches the ocean and pours into it, it becomes a delta of small rivers and streams, joining and separating in a maze of little watercourses, confused and multitudinous, but all existing because of the course of the great river.... Our best bet is to examine the myriad small streams, hoping that they will somehow tell us more about the river that fed them and the ultimate source."[65]

Crucified and Risen

Of course, there was probably more than one cause of Jesus' death. Not only might the countercultural nature of his teachings have contributed, but there may have been some confusion on the part of the leaders, especially the Romans, between the threat of revolt in the Maccabean style and the apocalyptic hope for God's intervention. It could also have been triggered by Jesus' statement that his followers would sit on thrones judging the twelve tribes of Israel. The theological claim that God gave him up to be crucified didn't come until much later, and it is impossible to find historically verifiable evidence for that kind of claim.

That his death was by crucifixion is, of course, confirmed by Tacitus' reference to "the extreme penalty."

The tradition of Jesus' resurrection from the dead may have its roots in a three-foot-tall stone tablet with eighty-seven lines of Hebrew in inked lettering. It was found around the end of the last century by a Jordanian peasant and later purchased from a Jordanian antiques dealer. Though some of the writing has been destroyed, and other parts are very dim and difficult to read, it appears to report traditions about the expected Messiah that were in circulation during the time of Jesus' life. It includes the claim that the Messiah would be resurrected after three days. The message on the stone purports to have been transmitted by the angel Gabriel. Scholars have determined that the stone dates from the late first century BCE.[66]

What does this mean? It is possible the narrative gospels might have used that ancient prophecy to validate their late claims for the divinity of Jesus. Certainly other prophecies were used to certify the messiahship and the divinity of Jesus, for example, that the Messiah would come from the house of David (tradition of his birth in Bethlehem) and the triumphal entry into Jerusalem (Zechariah 9:9).

This is not evidence for the resurrection, but it may well be part of the reason the resurrection stories were included in Paul's letters and the narrative gospels. In the meantime, the claim of bodily resurrection remains historically unverifiable and was roundly rejected by the Gnostic church. A recent publication has even sought to prove that Jesus survived the crucifixion.[67]

In sum, our knowledge of Jesus, his life, his teachings, and his end, is at best both sketchy and shaky. Even Q, though the nearest to the source, had first been written down from someone's memory and was then probably copied several times before Matthew and Luke could have used it. But for all that, the search for the historical Jesus persists.

Chapter 4

✦

How the Church Tried to Define Him

The lack of authoritative knowledge about Jesus and the tumultuous beginnings of the movement meant that if it was to have a future, many issues would have to be resolved and fixed for posterity. But that would require a process lasting some duration. It was a process that had already begun with the movement into Gentile territory and the spread of the theories developed in Paul's letters. It continued with the gradual separation of the Gentile cult from the Jewish Christian community. The loss of the Temple proved to be a crucial turning point. The break was complete by 100 CE. The Jewish Christians were disappearing, though some remnants appear to have lasted into the Middle Ages. The Jesus movement had lost its roots. What was left was the Gnostic church which still honored and taught the traditional teachings of Jesus, such as the *Gospel of Thomas*, and a number of Gentile groups, all contending for dominance.

So our story continues with the process by which the Paul-inspired movement came out of the fray; first as stronger than the Jewish Christian movement and Gnosticism, and second as a more or less unified and Constantine-certified institution.

Gnosticism as a Power

The rift between the Christian Jewish sect, and the breakaway movement which made the Jesus movement into a new cult in the Roman-Pagan world, was exacerbated by the growing Gnostic movement, which had arisen by the end of the first century. The earliest manifestation of the Gnostic strain of Christian belief had arisen out of an apparent conflict between the idea of Jesus as a spiritual being and the early Jewish belief that he was simply a member of the human family. While the idea of beings that were half human and half divine was common in that time and culture, the Docetic idea that Jesus only had the appearance of being a real, live human person began to take hold. This form of Christian belief seems to have begun in Asia Minor.

Gnosticism took the Docetic idea and developed a powerful new brand of Christian community. Along with the Docetic view of Jesus, it developed a theory of salvation through esoteric knowledge—that is, secret or hidden knowledge. So, like the earliest Jewish followers of Jesus had done, Gnostic Christians continued to focus on Jesus' teachings. For them, Jesus was the dispenser of saving wisdom.

As we have seen, Paul may even have been familiar with this notion of wisdom. The Gospel of John, much later, may betray the influence of Gnostic teaching when it talks about the pre-existent Jesus as the *logos,* the Greek word for the "wisdom," by which all things were created.

Gnosticism seems to have developed right alongside the development of what became the orthodox view of Jesus and salvation. Once again, it becomes apparent that Gnosticism was no more an intruder upon orthodoxy than orthodoxy was simply the final victor over Gnosticism.

It was a battle. Gnosticism took up verbal arms against the fleshly aspect of the earlier Jewish tradition of a wholly human, flesh-and-bones view of Jesus as an apocalyptic teacher. It also attacked the early institutionalization of Christianity, the focus on the blood of the martyrs, the blood of atonement, and the bodily resurrection of Jesus.

Among other issues being contested was the status of women in the church. During the earliest days of the movement, women were given leadership roles and were seated together with the men in worship. The Gnostics, for the most part, continued that tradition. They also honored the female wisdom and treated spirit as a female. But the Gentile church had begun to separate the women from the men by 100 CE, and its growing chauvinism was reflected in its attacks on the Gnostic church. In fact, the Montanists, a charismatic branch of the church, also had a place for women who were among its prophets. Tertullian, an early leader and theologian in the Gentile church, attacked them for that practice, but later became a Montanist himself.

Among the reasons for the struggle with the Marcionites (a pro-Paul, anti–Old Testament movement in the Gentile church), was their elevation of women to places of leadership. Tertullian also attacked them on these same grounds. He wrote, "It is not permitted for a woman to speak in the church, nor is it permitted for her to teach, nor to baptize, nor to offer [the Eucharist], nor for her to claim for herself a share in any *masculine* function—not to mention any priestly office."[68]

Ignatius and Polycarp took up their own verbal arms with writings specifically against Docetism. Marcus Aurelius, who lived between 121 and 180 CE, attacked the Gnosticism that had co-opted Docetism for its view of Jesus. This was a battle to the death—the eventual death of Gnosticism.

For Irenaeus, writing in 185 CE, it had not yet been resolved, nor would it be for another century or more. For many years, our knowledge of the Gnostic writings was confined to snippets from the writings of its critics, who knew those writings and characterized them in thoroughly negative terms.

However, Gnosticism also made the claim that it was the one "true church," and anathematized its opponents as an "imitation church."

The bitterness of these attacks on the "imitation church" probably indicate that they came from a late stage of the controversy. By the year 200 CE, the battle lines had been drawn. Both the orthodox Gentile Christians and Gnostic Christians claimed to represent the true church and accused one another of being outsiders, false brethren, and hypocrites.[69]

The writings of the early "Church Fathers" were preserved through their success in combating the Gnostic version of the Christian faith. However, most of the Gnostic documents themselves had been burned or buried. Many of those buried have only, in relatively recent years, been found and made available. Who knows how many more will come to light?

Thanks to the discovery of the fifty-three volumes of Gnostic and non-Gnostic documents in 1945, and more recent discoveries as well, we have many entire letters and gospels produced by the Gnostic church. I suggest you secure a copy of Bart Ehrman's book, *Lost Scriptures,* for the English text of many documents that were at some place and time, by some group of Jesus followers or other, used as sacred sources, and which may have been available for inclusion in our New Testament. Erhman's collection of texts includes seventeen gospels, five acts of the apostles, thirteen letters or related documents, seven apocalypses, and five different proposed lists of documents recommended for the final composition of the New Testament.

For those who have read the controversial novel *The Da Vinci Code*, it will be of interest to know that the Gnostic Gospel of Mary and Gospel of Philip, from which one of the characters quotes, reflect the view that Jesus had every appearance of being human since he was married to Mary Magdalene, with whom he had children. While making no claim to being historically accurate, the *Code* has opened up to the general public the whole field of writings and disputes in the early Jesus movement.

The understanding that Jesus was a real, live human being of flesh and blood was the original view of the Jesus movement. When did that change? How did Jesus become something quite different? The first influence was that of Paul's ignoring of the teachings of Jesus and their replacement by his focus on the death and resurrection of Jesus. The second powerful factor was the Docetism of the Gnostic church. While fighting Gnosticism tooth and nail, the Gentile church was, nevertheless, impacted by its Docetism. Even victors often adopt ideas and practices of the defeated. The struggle with Gnosticism continued through at least three centuries, and the question of who was Jesus was at the center of it all.

So here is the story.

The Origin of Christian scripture

When Paul wrote his letters, when the "Sayings Gospel Q" was composed, and when Mark and the other New Testament gospels were written, the only scripture was the law and the prophets of our present-day Old Testament. But eventually the Jesus movement came to develop its own sacred scripture.

This development is hardly surprising. Most religions have undergone a similar compulsion. By the second century, the break from the Jewish Jesus movement was complete. The movement was becoming a religion in its own right. Certain persons were assuming authority over specific geographical areas, and by midcentury they were claiming the title of bishops. A great many documents had already come out of the various contending branches of the church, and would continue to be produced for many years. This was natural because human beings seek to express their deepest feelings, and what Karen Armstrong calls their "transcendent experiences," in words. But, she notes, because "language has an inherent inadequacy, there is always something left unsaid, something that remains inexpressible."[70]

None of these early writings were written with the intent that they should become scripture. They all began as contemporary literature: letters, chronicles, propaganda, poetry, even myths. However, the very idea of sacred scripture implies that the documents thus designated are of a genre of literature different from any other genre. For example, when the author of 2 Peter commends Paul's letters to his readers, he is implying that they possess a certain special authority. Though he does not call them "scripture," he is already contributing to the process through which they would eventually be certified as sacred scripture.

So how does an ordinary document become "sacred scripture?" It does so when "people begin to treat it differently."[71] Certain writings are used ceremonially and thus acquire the reputation of being divinely inspired—of possessing a quality that communicates something more than the words themselves express. Armstrong describes the phenomenon as follows: "The Torah scroll is the most sacred object in the synagogue; enclosed in a precious covering, housed in an 'ark,' it is revealed at the climax of the liturgy when the scroll is conveyed formally around the congregation who touches it with the tassels of their prayer shawls ... Catholics also carry the Bible in procession, douse it with incense, and stand up when it is recited, making the sign of the cross on forehead, lips, and heart."[72]

Its sacred character arises from the way the documents are treated. For Jesus followers, the process may have begun when the letters of Paul were read in the house meetings. Other documents were also used in their meetings and their worship through the years and began to take on the aura of sacredness. The Gospels and non-Pauline letters now found in our New Testament, many of the treatises, letters, and gospels of the Gnostics, and the writings of Marcion and of Montanus, were among them. For certain congregations, each of these documents was in the process of becoming sacred literature well before any of them had been canonized. That is, they were read as though they were a different genre of literature. Most interpretations of these documents, both before and after the canon was established, were allegorical and poetic. And there was no official canon, or list of books, that was supposed to be treated as sacred scripture until the end of the fourth century. Neither was there any notion that God had literally inspired the authors until the nineteenth century.

The first church leader to suggest the idea of a Christian scripture was Barnabas (not Paul's colleague) in 131 CE. But the first one to actually propose what it should contain was Marcion. He had come from the Black Sea vicinity, by way of Ephesus, to Rome where he became a teacher in the Christian community there. He saw himself as a reformer of the Gentile church. In the first place, he was a Docetist. In the second place, he wanted to call the Gentile church back to its Pauline heritage from which he felt it was straying. He was concerned about what he saw as Judaizing tendencies and he preferred Paul's treatment of the Jesus tradition. He was trying to combine his Docetism with his understanding of Paul. Any who abandoned Paul, he took to be traitors to the cause. In fact, this was probably the first instance of the Jesus movement using the idea of heresy.

Marcion could not accept the God of the Old Testament, believing that its God was inferior to the God of Jesus. Therefore, he believed the movement should abandon the Jewish scriptures entirely and create its own canon. So his list was composed of the Gospel of Luke and eleven letters attributed to Paul. The Gospels of Mark, Matthew, and John were already in use in many of the churches, and their exclusion doomed Marcion's list. The consensus was that any claim that Jesus was the Messiah required the messianic promises of the prophets for substantiation. Besides, both Paul and the gospels already written cited the Jewish scriptures as authoritative. Marcion's list was rejected, he was excommunicated, and he died shortly thereafter in 144 CE. Nevertheless, the churches he founded continued to exist for some time as thorns in the side of the Gentile Christian community, thus further splintering the Jesus movement during the second century CE. Furthermore, Marcion's Docetism was anathema. So the Gentile Christian community was already flexing its muscles.

Another movement appeared in 156 CE to challenge both Gnosticism and the existing Gentile church. It became known as Montanism, after its founder Montanus. Montanus suddenly came on the scene with his charismatic prophesying. It was not a new phenomenon in the church, since Paul had to deal with it in the middle of the first century, but Montanus claimed that through the gift of prophecy he had direct access to God's revelations. Sometimes the Montanists seemed to challenge the favorite teachings of those rising to positions of authority. One of the most controversial ideas of the Montanists was that Jesus' second coming was imminent. This return to an early Pauline teaching didn't set well, but gained a troublesome following.

Near the end of the second century CE, the first Christian philosopher, Clement, showed up in Alexandria, Egypt, where he started his own school. He came either from Asia Minor or from Greece, where he had studied Platonic philosophy. He introduced Platonic thought into his theories about Jesus, God, and salvation, but he was not a Gnostic. Rather, he made the introduction of Greek concepts into Christian theology an accepted practice in the Gentile church. This practice represented a further removal of the church from its Jewish roots.

The first systematic theologian, Origen, was greatly influenced by Clement and also lived in Alexandria. With the development of systematic theology, Jewish ways of thinking were largely eradicated, and with it, any hope of recovering the real, Jewish, peasant teacher of the early Jesus movement.

All the while, Gnosticism remained a powerful alternative to the Paul-inspired trajectory of what was to become orthodoxy. But by the second half of the second century, the followers of Jesus began to think of themselves as "another race," neither Jewish nor Gentile, but Christian.[73] By the end of the century, the first use of the word "catholic," as applied to the church, came into being.

In the meantime, there was still no Christian scripture. However, a list of books finally appeared that matched our present New Testament contents. It was called the "Muratorian Canon." Though a fair representation of much non-Gnostic Christian worship at the time, it had not yet been officially adopted.

The Council of Nicea

The conflicts and controversies, the anathemas and heresies, the debates and arguments had, by now, been raising dust all over the Roman Empire. The Jewish Jesus sects, known as the Ebionites, and the Nazarenus, along with the Gentile sect *cum* cult and the rise of Docetism and its child the Christian Gnostic movement, were all contenders for dominance by the end of the first century CE. Then there appeared within the Gentile Christian movement the rise of the Marcionite churches and, following them, the Montanist churches, all with their own interpretations of the faith. Who was Jesus really? Everybody had their opinions and each branch of the Jesus movement sought converts and dominance.

Already, persecution by the Caesars on the one hand and, on the other hand, the desire for martyrdom by many of the Gentile believers, such as Polycarp, Marcus Aurelius, and other true believers, were feeding on each other. Without the persecution, martyrdom would have had no way to exist. Martyrdom was seen as the way by which one could find fellowship with the crucified Jesus, and thus achieve salvation

The desire for a sacred scripture also represented an effort to resist the increasing pressure from the Caesars. The newly discovered need to make a case for the new faith produced a group of "apologists," who were those who wrote rational explanations of the faith.[74] One of the earliest apologists was Justin (100–160 CE). He was greatly impressed with the Gospel of John and its reference to *logos*. For Justin, *logos*, also translated as "word" or "reason," combined with *pneuma*, translated as "spirit," constituted the meaning of "God." And this God had been incarnate in Jesus of Nazareth. It was, therefore, God as known in Jesus of Nazareth who was also present at the beginning of all things and was the reality behind every teaching in the Old Testament, as well as the inspiration for Hebrews, Greeks, and Romans. Therefore, everything was to be interpreted as a manifestation of the "spirit" and "reason," which were incarnate in Jesus. This argument was calculated to appeal to the Greek and pagan worlds. It became central to the interpretations of the theologians who have come to be known as the "Church Fathers." The seminal ideas that became the doctrinal basis of orthodoxy were thus sowed by Justin and the Gospel of John. Those ideas were the doctrine of the incarnation of God in the flesh of Jesus of Nazareth and, therefore, the doctrine of the "preexistence of Christ." Thereby the title "Christ," as the original translation of "Messiah," was made to signify a kind of metaphysical reality entirely different from its original meaning. Though modified by Greek concepts, it was a continuation of the trajectory initiated by Paul in the first century.

As a result of Justin's apologetic, many theologians adopted the practice of developing allegories out of Old Testament scripture. Thus, they claimed to have reached behind the literal words of scripture to uncover the real meaning intended by the *logos*. Origen, the first systematic theologian of the Jesus movement, made consistent use of allegory in composing his systematic theological treatise called *Of First Principles*. It was not an easy thing to persuade the pagan world that this Jewish peasant could have any meaning for them.

But this also meant that the very existence of the Christian movement was under increasing threat. According to historian Karen Armstrong, "Before the conversion of Constantine in 312, it seemed unlikely that Christianity would survive, as Christians were subjected to sporadic but intense persecution by the Roman authorities. Once they had made it clear that they were no longer members of the synagogue, the Romans regarded the church as a *superstitio* of fanatics, who had committed the cardinal sin of impiety by breaking with the parent faith."[75]

The problem was that, by this time, the influence of Greek thought had overwhelmed the ancient Jewish view of reality and had divided the world into a divine realm and a material, created realm. God occupied the divine realm and human beings the created realm. Sounds a bit like Plato, doesn't it? How to bridge the gap between the two realms had become the question. This had never been an issue among the Jews, but by the beginning of the fourth century, it raised new questions about where Jesus fit into the scheme of things.

For the Gnostics, with their Docetic view of Jesus as a spiritual being who only gave the appearance of being a flesh and blood human, one could become divine like Jesus by following his secret teachings. Thus, the gap between divine and human was not seen by them as problematic. By the end of the first century CE, Gnosticism had become a powerful presence in the Jesus movement and Church Fathers were often more noted for their diatribes against the Gnostics than for their positive contributions to the development of Christian doctrine.

However, some of the leaders of the Gentile church also became active proponents of special theories. One of them was Athanasius of Alexandria. His most vocal opponent was a charismatic and handsome presbyter in the church in Alexandria by the name of Arias. Athanasius claimed that the only way Jesus could represent the human race before God required that he be both human and divine at the same time. But Arias, believing that such a creature was impossible, taught that Jesus was a third kind of being, somewhere between divine and human. In this way, Jesus provided a bridge between God and man. Both men began to gain powerful followings in the Roman Empire.

This was, of course, but one of the disputes raised by the question of how to bridge the gap. The debates became so rancorous that it affected the whole Jesus movement, and had even become a common topic of discussion and argument among the common people.

So, when Constantine came to power in Rome and converted to Christianity, he had two major problems on his hands. First, what could he himself believe about Jesus? So many claimants to the truth made a secure faith almost impossible. That was his personal problem. His political problem, however, proved to be the tipping point. He needed far more unity among his subjects than was possible with the raging battles among the Christians. So at the peak of the struggle between the Arians and the Athanasians, he determined to put an end to the chaos and settle the question once and for all about who Jesus really was. That way both his personal problem and his political problem could be resolved in one fell swoop.

In the year 325 CE, Constantine called a council of the leaders of the Christian communities together in Nicea, in modern Turkey, to determine the correct answer to the questions which raged about Jesus' identity and function. The council would be known to history as the Council of Nicea.

So what happened at Nicea? Well, the debate was joined, principally, between the Athanasians and the Arians. At the end, it was decided in favor of Athanasius, and Arius was excommunicated as a heretic. The church had spoken, and the truth was decided. Jesus was God, constituted of the same substance as the Father, but he was also human. Perhaps, one could say that his inner reality was divine just like the Father, but his outer reality was human just like you or me. Sounds a little like Justin all over again. In either case, it was said that the bridge had been crossed. The original Jewish view of Jesus as an inspired teacher and prophet was dead. Neither did he simply have the appearance of a flesh and blood human being as the Docetic Gnostics had it. God had actually become incarnate; that is, God inhabited the body of the human Jesus. So Jesus was both divine and human. Therefore, both the Arians and the Gnostics were finally and definitively ousted from the church.

So the Father and the Son were said to both be of the same substance, and belief in the Holy Spirit was added at the end of the creed, which Athanasias wrote following the council meeting. The final form of this creed was adopted at the Council of Constantinople in 381 CE. At this council meeting, the Holy Spirit was affirmed to be also of the same substance as the Father and the Son, thus fixing the doctrine of the Trinity. Nicea's version, as recorded by Athanasias, states, "We believe in one God, the Father Almighty, maker of all things visible and invisible and in the Lord, Jesus Christ, the Son of God, the only begotten of the Father, that is, of the same substance as the Father, ... of one substance with the Father, through whom all things were made ... who for us men and for our salvation came down and was made man ... And we believe in the Holy Spirit."

It satisfied Constantine, who was no theologian himself, but the wrangling in the church has never ceased. In fact, Athanasius himself was later excommunicated more than once, and many of the bishops continued to teach their own earlier beliefs. The Arian churches continued to exist for another sixty years. What was established at Nicea and Constantinople was what we now know as orthodoxy. Orthodoxy is coupled with heterodoxy. That is, whoever did not adopt the views established by the Council of Nicea and subsequent councils of the church was declared to be heterodox, or a heretic.[76] Up until that time, many leaders in the church had written against the "heresies" of the Judaizers, the Gnostics, the Marcionites, and the Montanists. But now there was a standard by which heresy could be firmly and precisely determined. The church as a thoroughly Gentile institution with its standards of belief, its hierarchical authority, and its institutional organization had become "established."

That is how the church defined the historical Jesus out of existence. Of course, he had already been, in large part, lost from view, but now his reentry was also barred. The persecutions had ceased and martyrdom had lost its rationale, but the foundation of the infamous Inquisition had been laid.

The Course of Establishment

Establishment can be said to have occurred when Constantine gave his approval to the work of Nicea, but the church had a long way to go before it would become a full-fledged institution.

The full-blown doctrine of the Trinity had to wait until the Council of Constantinople in 381 CE. The Muratorian Canon had been proposed much earlier, but debate continued for another two hundred years before it received an official stamp of approval by the Council of Carthage in 394 CE. Candidates for inclusion were many. Many of the Gnostic writings were still available, notably the *Gospel of Thomas*, plus the works of Marcion and Montanus, and a multitude of others. However, in the meantime, many of the controversial writings had been burned or hidden away, and their authors anathematized by those who were gaining power and influence in the Jesus movement.

It is clear that at least two major criteria were functioning in the decisions that were made. First, the closer the authors were to Jesus the more weight the material had. This criterion remains in current historiography. Although multiple sources were used in some cases in the process, it is not clear that this was a functioning criterion. This explains, in part, why there were so many letters, gospels, and other documents falsely attributed to the disciples and other early leaders of the movement. We know that most authorship was manufactured to lend credence to the content.

The second criterion was how well the content of these documents met the orthodox criteria set by Nicea and Constantinople. This criterion ignores the requirements of independent sources and of lack of bias which are essential to modern historiographical practice.

A third, very practical, factor was also at work. How wide was the support each choice had across the movement? For example, Marcion had wanted to include only Luke, but there were other gospels also available for inclusion. Some parts of the church still liked the Gospel of Mark, others preferred Matthew, Luke, or John. Some liked Thomas, and the Gnostic communities preferred still other gospels. Therefore, no single gospel could have satisfied the disparate branches and sectors of the Gentile church. Four were chosen. Thomas obviously did not represent the orthodox view. John did. The others were close enough. And, of course, the "Sayings Gospel Q" came along with Matthew and Luke.

Besides the letters of Paul that Marcion had included in his list, a large number of other letters ascribed to Paul and some of the apostles had appeared and were available for inclusion. But even after the action of the Council of Carthage, many churches continued to use the literature they had been using for many years. In fact, some Gnostic gospels were still being used in churches during the Middle Ages, but the line had been drawn.

During this same period, the Jesus movement had moved out of the homes and synagogues where it had worshipped and studied. Church buildings were constructed and began to adopt the architectural styles of the period and country in which they were built. Clerical garb was designed and worn and the hierarchy evolved.

The authority of those who were called bishops was institutionalized as that which was bestowed through a supposed unbroken succession of the laying on of hands from the first disciples onward. This theory was already being promoted by some authorities early in the second century.

Authority in the Jesus movement in the earliest days was exercised by charismatic personalities. That is how the sects of the first century operated. But gradually, as the sects morphed into cultic status, the need to institutionalize authority arose and continued to evolve into the fourth and fifth centuries. The establishment of the church under Constantine made the institutionalization of the church that much easier and, in fact, ended the cult status of the Gentile church.

This process was also probably necessary. Without it, orthodoxy could never have developed, heresy would never have been heard of, and it is quite possible that we would never have heard the name "Jesus" in the twenty-first century. The Jesus movement might well have seeped away like water into the sand.

In any case, we have lost the man, Jesus of Nazareth. The barest facts are known about him, and only a set of teachings, probably sometimes ill-remembered, often edited, and only tenuously connected to the man, remain.

What can we do with so little?

PART II

Chapter 5

✦

What Can We Do with Him Now?

We are not sure what Jesus said, and we do not know all he did. We only have a story woven of many strands and composed of many memories and many dreams. It is a story sometimes confused because it is always colored by the expectations and prejudices of those who reported it. There is little sure history in the varied reports, except that he lived in Roman Palestine, gathered followers, and died there, almost certainly on a Roman cross.

So, if we can't know the historical Jesus, either his actual identity or exactly what he said and didn't say, must we simply close our eyes, reach back, and grab the old assumption that those who chose which gospels would be included in the New Testament canon had some direct line to God who whispered into their spiritual ear which books he had inspired?

Or ought we try to open the canon and add those writings we especially like among the millions that have been produced in the centuries since the canon was closed? No, we cannot be so foolish as to think that would solve our problem even if it were possible.

So what are we to do? Given the limits of our sure knowledge and the tentative status of the probabilities, we can take the simple, logical course and give him up entirely—simply chop ourselves free from the traditions about Jesus altogether, entirely dismiss him from our spiritual understanding and delete him from our faith. On the other hand, we remember what the church has always done—it has settled for a Jesus of its own shaping, and so can we.

The clue to this option can be found in the seminal work on the historical Jesus authored by Albert Schweitzer in 1906. In his landmark work *The Quest of the Historical Jesus*, he wrote, "The truth is, it is not Jesus as historically known, but Jesus as spiritually arisen with men, who is significant for our time and can help it. Not the historical Jesus, but the spirit which goes forth from Him and in the spirits of men strives for new influence and rule, is that which overcomes the world."[77]

Thus Schweitzer closed his book, not with his own image of Jesus, but with an open ended kind of invitation.

Nevertheless, he expressed his concern that the "world-negating" message of Jesus' teachings might be lost if we abandoned the historical search. But we shall not lose it because we will still claim the countercultural message of the Q material.

We have the story; we have the tradition, though most of it is nonhistorical. We have absorbed that tradition into our bones beginning perhaps when, as children, we stood up in Sunday School every week and sang at the top of our lungs, "Jesus loves me, this I know, for the Bible tells me so." We cannot escape him. We are hooked on Jesus, and we have been so for the last two thousand years. In every century, we've found a different Jesus, each time with limited connection to the historical person and often with small connection to the biblical tradition about him. Each time, he has come alive all over again through the image that has been created. If it has worked for all those Jesus lovers through the ages, let's see if it will work for us.

Creating the Jesus We Need

In *Jesus Through the Centuries*, Jaroslav Pelikan confirms Schweitzer's view by identifying and describing the images which symbolize the shifting perceptions of Jesus as Western society has changed since his time. I want to identify Pelikan's images here, along with a few of my own qualifying observations.

The basic image of Jesus that dominated first-century Judaism, says Pelikan, was that of a rabbi or teacher. How historical is this image? If the Q theory is correct, then I believe the content of Q to be as near to a historical view of him as we will come, and he was indeed, before all else, a teacher or rabbi. It was certainly the image held by those who

knew him and remembered him after his death. It was the image held
by the Roman soldiers who first heard stories about him from their
Jewish subjects. As we have seen, his teachings about the Kingdom
seem to have made the Kingdom into a verb rather than a noun, and
every observance of Jesus' teachings by his followers was a further
realization of the Kingdom coming. It was also the way of salvation.

In the Jesus movement of the late first and second centuries, the
primary image was that of the "Turning Point in History." That is,
it was a further adaptation of the old Jewish apocalyptic expectation
that treated him as the herald of the coming Kingdom. The old age
of the law had passed, and the new age of the Spirit had begun, thus
constituting a turning point in history. To set your mind on the things
of the Spirit was the way of holiness. This message appears to have been
spread especially by Paul.

But later, during the second century, says Pelikan, the focus began
to shift to Jesus as the "Light to the Gentiles." In point of fact, this shift
had begun earlier and had precipitated the final break with Judaism
which had occurred by 100 CE. This marked the rise of the Gentile
church, which persisted throughout the third century. Paul was the
primary forerunner of this shift as well.

The influence of Greek thought on the teachings of the church
during the third and fourth centuries created the "Cosmic Christ" as
the *logos*, or wisdom of God. The term "cosmic" distinguishes Christ,
as the Greek translation of the "Messiah" of the Jews, from the Christ
who was a universal reality from the creation of the world forward. The
Gospel of John, written around the end of the first century, had already
introduced the Greek concepts of *logos* and of the preexistent Christ
who participated in the creation of the world along with God himself.
The cosmic Christ, however, became much further developed through
Justin and the councils of the church which followed. The Councils
of Nicea and Constantinople during the fourth century, for example,
continued to introduce Greek concepts into the growing orthodoxy of
the time. Salvation came, more and more, to be a matter of believing
the correct things.

In the meantime, the confrontation of the early church with the
rule of Caesar during the fourth century produced a new image of
Jesus as the "King of Kings," according to Pelikan. The idea of Jesus
as the king may have originated from the Jewish title for their kings,

which was "Messiah." However, this was also the period during which Constantine ruled and gave official status to the Gentile church. Perhaps this newfound approval suggested that Jesus was, after all, superior to all other rulers. In any case, the image of Jesus as the King of Kings came to exercise great influence and remains a part of our contemporary tradition.

Augustine's work in the fifth century was instrumental in creating Jesus as the "Son of Man." Thus, a new light was focused on sin and human possibilities that lasted through the sixth and seventh centuries. In this image, the attention was shifted from the esoteric, cosmic Christ and the King of Kings to a concern with the existential struggles of humankind. And Jesus' role as a human being loomed larger.

However, throughout the eighth and ninth centuries, Byzantine art and architecture highlighted the "Iconic Images of Jesus" as a symbol of the divinity behind the human aspect of Jesus. Obviously this emphasis had no direct connection to Docetism, but it did refocus the image of Jesus on the eternal and cosmic proportions of the orthodox view of the incarnation, effectively reasserting the Greek concepts lying behind orthodoxy.

The tenth and eleventh centuries, says Pelikan, saw the literature and art of the Middle Ages focused on the "Crucified Jesus" as the means of salvation. To be sure, the suffering of Jesus on the cross had been preeminent in Paul's teaching. However, subsequent shifts in imagery had sometimes moved away from that focus, as we have just seen.

The eleventh and twelfth centuries found the rise of the monastic movement in which the imitation of the "Ascetic Jesus" seemed to rule. Not only did the image of Jesus take on a new appearance, but the means of salvation also radically changed. That is, one's salvation came to depend on a participation in Jesus' style of life by imitating the asceticism of his chastity, poverty, etc. This idea of salvation through imitation of Jesus is reminiscent of the much earlier longing of many Christians for martyrdom as a means of participating in Jesus' suffering. Of course, that possibility had long since passed when the Romans ceased killing Christians.

Pelikan identifies the "Bridegroom of the Soul" as representing the thirteenth century, the "Divine and Human Model," as manifested by Francis of Assisi, as marking the fourteenth century, and the "Universal

Man" of Erasmus, the prototypical Renaissance man, representing the fifteenth and sixteenth centuries.

The "Mirror of the Eternal" was often used by both the Reformation and Roman Catholic leaders in the seventeenth century, while a reaction to the Crusades raised the image of the "Prince of Peace" during the eighteenth century. The eighteenth century also saw the rise of the "Teacher of Common Sense" image of Jesus and the enlightenment search for the historical Jesus.

Under the influence of the Romantic Movement and philosophical idealism, the image of Jesus in the nineteenth century became the "Poet of the Spirit." Emerson called him "the bard of the Holy Ghost." The twentieth century saw the coming of Jesus the "Liberator" with the appearance of such figures as Gandhi and Martin Luther King, Jr., and now, in the twentieth and twenty-first centuries, we have "the Man Who Belongs to the World."[78]

Within the Christian tradition, it is apparent that the image of Jesus that one holds has a great deal to do with one's understanding of how one can be "saved," whether by following certain teachings and practices, trusting the atonement, or believing the doctrines.

Pelikan's work consists in placing each image in its historical context, both cultural and philosophical. His assumption is that none of these images make any serious claim to represent the historical reality of Jesus of Nazareth, except the first. Indeed, I suspect that every individual within each epoch is influenced, not only by the ethos of his own time, but also by the unique experiences of his own life, when and if he thinks of Jesus at all.

Schweitzer suggests that this is the only way Jesus can come alive. Given the missing history of Jesus, I believe this to be true.

How Can We Build Our New Image?

None of the images we have just discussed were built from a deliberate decision to create something different. They arose out of a combination of three sources. First, they were influenced by the traditions they had inherited. As for us, we can also read the tradition in the pages of the New Testament and study the noncanonical works which the New Testament canon rejected. We have done some of that study in the preceding chapters. Second, they reflected the culture of the times. That is, the changing philosophical, sociological, theological, and political tendencies of the age had to be respected. We ourselves have already been formed in a significant measure by our culture. Third, they were somehow responsive to the existential questions they were forced to ask by the universal needs they continued to experience. [77] What remains for us, in the next paragraphs, is to illustrate how the universal needs which all of us have just by being human, force us to ask questions that demand new answers.

For example, understanding is one of our universal needs. In my case, it is the need for understanding who God is that has led to this inquiry. But what is more important is that the search has also been highly personal.

As a pastor, I have heard a thousand questions from people who can't understand why God behaves in the way he apparently does. With them, I have struggled to make sense of their circumstances. More often than not, I have simply failed. It is true that many times I have been able to help somebody feel a bit better. They may have only needed someone to listen who could understand the pain in their questions. But my answers have rarely satisfied me and, often enough, have failed to satisfy my questioners.

Here is a sampling that you may recognize.

Question: "Pastor, why did God take my son at such an early age?"

My answer: "God didn't do it. It was the driver of the truck who went to sleep because he hadn't rested the required number of hours the night before."

"I know, but why did God let him do that? He could have made him sleep more."

So I say: "But God's not like that."

"But he should be. He's supposed to be good. I don't understand."

Or here's another:

"Genocide! I saw the pictures on television. I can't believe God would countenance anything like that. It's horrible! I just can't believe in God anymore."

Now, what can I say? Finally, I say: "I don't believe in that kind of God any more either."

So, I have an existential problem. It's not merely an intellectual problem. It has touched my soul! What kind of God can I believe in now?

I proceed to reflect on my problem. I start to do what I once learned to do when I was a teenager and read Charles Sheldon's *In His Steps* (*What Would Jesus Do?*). I begin to ask that question. But how do I know what Jesus would do? I don't even know who he was, what he was like, what he did, or with any certainty, what he said. So I have another existential problem. It's very personal, because over the years I have become enamored of Jesus, or at least of the tradition about Jesus.

Naturally, I want to know what kind of God the historical Jesus believed in. One would assume that, as a man of his own times, he must have believed in the God of his fathers. That would be the one God who had delivered his ancestors from captivity in Egypt, who had given the Ten Commandments to Moses, and who had liberated the people from their captivity in Babylon and Syria. But if Robinson is correct about Jesus' message reported in Q, then Jesus understood God to be the one who was doing the miracles of healing and actually manifesting his reign in every act of compassion and every merciful deed that Jesus performed. And through his teachings, Jesus was calling on his followers to do likewise.

Thereby, Jesus seems to have collapsed two related but separate things into one thing. The first, God's initiative, was the apocalyptic promise that God would intervene in history to save Israel from its oppressors. The second, the people's responsibility, was that the Jews needed to take action for their own freedom by rebelling violently against the oppressor. But Jesus seemed to be teaching that the miracles of healing and the acts of turning the other cheek, etc., were themselves the acts of God intervening through his people who were, at the same time, taking responsibility for obeying his teachings.

Jesus' teachings were instructions for the people's cooperation with God. The implication being that when they were compassionate and loving and self-effacing, it was God who was doing it through them. They were already participants in the reigning of God—the coming of his Kingdom.

Now, I take that to be a pretty strong clue that Jesus' God was somehow different from the God he'd inherited. He was neither a God of invincible power, nor was he a God who overrides the freedom of his subjects. He was not a God who intervened by fiat. He was a God who worked through his children. And what he worked were the works of compassion, selflessness, and a special kind of love which we call grace.

We don't know what Jesus' theology was. That is, we don't know what his definition of "God" was. We only know that he probably said that these acts of mercy and love were like yeast. They worked slowly, even invisibly, and the Kingdom was inexorably "a-comin' in." His was a different kind of God than the traditional God who would appear in some sudden, violent intervention in history to overthrow the oppressor.

If this is all true, then Jesus was already changing the definition of "God." He already had a new vision of God. So, still not knowing with historical certainty just what Jesus taught, I take my clue from this account of his message. I, like the earliest followers of Jesus, see him as a teacher. But, unlike the Gnostics, I see him as a real flesh-and-blood Jewish peasant who had a world-changing vision of who God is and how he works. He is not the only begotten Son of God, like John and the Nicean Creed have it, but he was a child of God just like all of us are. That is why, when he or we do the works of compassion, deeds of reconciliation, and acts of healing, God is also creating his Kingdom. He is reigning.

I must, therefore, reject the notions of the the Gnostics, the Arians, the Athanasians, and the orthodox Gentile church who treat Jesus as a different species of being. Rather, I want to take my clues from Q's version to construct my image of Jesus. He was not a separate species of being; rather, he was a straight forward human being. He did not die his death to pay some debt I have accrued. He died as the result of his faithfulness to himself and to God. His resurrection story is not to be seen as the proof of a blissful life in eternity, but as the promise of a further journey.

So far, so good. But we need more than suggestions as to what God is not, and an idea of the kinds of things he is doing. We need a new vision of who God is if we are to respond satisfactorily to the kinds of questions my parishioners often asked—to say nothing of satisfying my own desire to better understand. It doesn't help a lot to say, as I have often heard it said, "Who knows the mind of God? He knows what he's doing. So relax and let God," or even "Just have faith."

Therefore, based on the clues provided by the "Sayings Gospel Q," I need to set forth more definitively some propositions about God and his relation to this world. It is necessary to remember that these propositions do not pretend to describe either the classical view of theism or Jesus' inherited view of God, but rather to define a God and his relation to the world which is implied by my understanding of Jesus' revised definition suggested by the Q document.

Propositions about God and the World

This will be brief and fairly succinct. You will find a fuller development of these ideas in my book *A New Vision of God for the 21st Century.*

God is all spirit and all spirit is God.

The concept of spirit is central here. But what is spirit? For my purposes, I take my idea of spirit from the only place where we all experience spirit from the inside—in our own self-awareness. Self-awareness is the phenomenon of being aware of "I" as an individual distinct from everything that is not "I." Wherever there is self-awareness, there is spirit. And wherever there is spirit, there is God. We start with that much.

Every self-aware spirit, whether human or otherwise, is like an organ in the spiritual body of God.

This is an analogy that suggests three things: 1) that every one of us is a part of God since we are self-aware spirits and all spirit is God; (2) that God, as self-aware spirit, is the Head of the whole collection of spirits; and 3) that every self-aware spirit is in communication with every other spirit, analogous to the communication among cells which goes on within the nervous system of our own physical bodies. This manifests itself, minimally and sporadically, in various forms of extrasensory perception.

The Head (God's own self-awareness) of his/her own spiritual body is seeking to heal all her/his parts.

There are ills and malfunctions of the spiritual organs in God's spiritual body, analogous to the ills and malfunctions of organs in our physical bodies. God is always striving to heal the wounds and ills in the organs of her/his spiritual body as we strive to heal our own physical bodies.

God and we are either in constant cooperation with one another or in opposition to one another.
We either strive for our healing (and therefore God's healing since we are part of his spiritual body), or resist God's pressure and permit the ills and disharmonies within ourselves (and therefore within God). God always works by putting spiritual pressure on us while leaving us, as self-aware spirits, to cooperate or resist. She/he forces nothing!

Assuming this to be a reasonable definition of who God is in relation to his/her children, we cannot blame God for not doing what we would expect God to do if he/she were the kind of God we grew up believing in, or for doing what we wouldn't expect him/her to do if God were that kind of God. Rather, we are simply responsible for doing whatever we can to work healing in ourselves, in others, in the world and, therefore, in God the Spirit herself/himself.

What Does This Mean for Our Image of Jesus?

We cannot pretend our image of Jesus will be historical. We just don't know enough about him. We have to be realistic about what the New Testament is, and we have to understand that it is not history. History requires us to set aside our prejudices and our hopes. As Bart Ehrman makes clear, history is confined to those facts for which there is compelling evidence. Therefore, there is very little of history in the images through which the Christian world has seen Jesus across the centuries.

However, our picture of Jesus will build upon those few historical facts that scholars have established but, like everyone else, we will bring our imagination to bear upon those facts. However, we dare not allow it to run wild, but must direct it to serve those universal needs which every human being possesses by reason of his being human.[79] That is to say, we are attempting to create an image of Jesus which can speak to those needs. That is exactly what the Ebionites and Nazarenos, the Marcionites and the Montanists, were doing. And that is what both the Gnostics and their enemies, the orthodox Gentiles, sought to do. They all created a Jesus to meet their own perceived needs.

That means our image of Jesus, like theirs, will also be mythical. It does not preclude, however, that we may use selected features of the tradition about him, such as his role and message as a teacher, his personal encounter with God, and the fiction of his physical resurrection, as well as the historical facts and probabilities of his humanity, his birth, and his death. We know the following. Jesus was born in Nazareth of Galilee in Roman Palestine somewhere between 4 and 7 BCE by the Gregorian calendar (historical). Mary and Joseph were his parents (probable). Joseph and Jesus both worked in the construction trades (speculative). Jesus left home to become an itinerant teacher following his baptism by John (probable). He taught that God's reign (Kingdom) was to be seen in every act of healing, compassion, and self-abnegation (probable). He ran afoul of the authorities who feared his popularity and possible political repercussions (probable). He was crucified somewhere between 27 and 29 CE by the Gregorian calendar (historical). That's about it. But this information at least grounds him in history as a Jewish peasant man.

That is why we simply cannot treat him as the *only* begotten son of God, for we are all equally begotten by God. It does mean that we are free to use the sayings in Q as the essential teachings of our mythical teacher, even though their total accuracy cannot be proven. It means we cannot treat his death as an atonement for sins because God didn't do it. It was carried out by powerful leaders who were acting out of ignorance, in spite of the efforts of the Head (see above propositions about God) to point them in a different direction. Probably, they didn't like the countercultural teachings of his "beatitudes"—his inversion of the values by which the society of his time lived. Perhaps they confused the apocalyptic hope of the people and the growing passion for revolt, and so saw him as a threat to peace in the empire. In any case, their ignorance meant they were not in tune with the Head of the world of spirit, so they found a way to get rid of him. Our image of him doesn't have to include crucifixion on a cross, or execution by a rifle squad, or even poison in his food—but only that they thought they had dealt with the problem by getting rid of him.

But he comes back to haunt them and to corroborate the truth of his teachings about what God needs us to do and be.

Salvation doesn't mean being saved from damnation. It means becoming fully human, as our image of Jesus is fully human, and therefore becoming divine as he became divine. His teachings are our guide in that process. We are to learn to weep over those who suffer, who destroy and divide, and to laugh with those who revel in God's gifts and presence. The bedrock of his teaching appears to be the promises set forth in the Beatitudes. Of them Erik Kolbell says, "Each is a poetic and exquisitely paradoxical meditation on how to live a life of faith in a world of doubt. In lilting beauty and fluid verse, the Beatitudes sanctify those qualities in us that are the very antithesis of success as we in the West have come to understand (and pursue) it."[80]

What a different world it would be if such values as meekness, mercy, peace, love of God, and hunger after righteousness constituted its value system.

Finally, it means that what we humans have begun in the nest of our earthly life, we will be given the opportunity to continue when we have left the nest and its limitations and become free as we have never been free before—free to grow into perfect communion with our Head, the Spirit who is God.

Jesus as the Pioneer of Our Faith

When I think of this particular Jesus as my hero and my ideal, I am deeply moved. Of course, I am also sometimes caught up in the exploits of a celebrity, and my enthusiasm can move me to read all about him and I can't get enough of him/her. I may admire this celebrity for his talents and his performances. For me, it is likely to be a star athlete, an author, or even a politician. But I have no wish to imitate him. I might think of how great it would be to have been so accomplished, and I might even have imagined what it would be like to be so admired. But a celebrity is one thing, and a hero is something else altogether. Joseph Campbell describes the classic hero: "A hero ventures forth from the world of common clay into a region of supernatural wonder. Fabulous forces are there encountered and a decisive victory is won. The hero comes back from this mysterious adventure with the power to bestow boons on his fellow man."[81]

A celebrity does not change my life, my hero does. My hero speaks to me and tells me about my possibilities.

Once upon a time, many years ago, my hero was Popeye. He had huge muscles and could send his enemies flying with a single blow.

That's what I wanted to be able to do when a bully attempted repeatedly to pick a fight with me during recess. So I idolized Popeye and resolved to become strong just like him. I did not imagine that Popeye really existed, but that did not matter. I had my picture of him, and the comic strips told their stories about his adventures. I thought of him as my hero. Therefore, I idealized him and sought to emulate him. Because he ate spinach by the can full, I asked my mama to give me spinach every day. The fact is that I learned to love spinach. To this day I love spinach.

Something like that is what it means to have a hero. A hero often has some connection to reality so that one can identify him with some historical figure, such as Hercules, Columbus, Abraham Lincoln, or even Martin Luther King, Jr. A hero has always collected certain mythic characteristics which ignore the historic reality, and there are features of the historic life of the individual which are simply forgotten, while his most admirable qualities are exalted to mythic proportions. His actual history is not so important. What is important is the image that we have of him, and that image tends to project the ideals which we would like to embody ourselves. Because the hero embodies the desirable qualities, he becomes not only the object of our adoration and love, but also the ideal which forms the goal of our lives. We all need a hero.

Jesus, as hero, tells me about his encounter with God—what God has told him and sent him to do for others. So he meets our needs in something more than a rational way. It's not merely a sentimental journey, but our emotions brilliantly color it and our way is lighted.

As we saw in our survey of images, the stories about Jesus have served to provide both a hero and an ideal for those who have called themselves Christians for the last twenty centuries.

Just look at some of the names that have been used to refer to this one whose stories we have heard and loved all our lives. The names themselves all say something about the image that is projected.

Messiah (anointed one)
Immanuel (God with us)
Savior (future security)
Lord (commander)
Lamb of God (sacrifice of atonement)
Bright and Morning Star (herald of a new day)

Lily of the Valley (beauty of character)
Bread of Life (nourishment for the sprit)
Light of the World (illumination for the way)
The Son of Man (Jesus' own words according to John, in refutation of the Docetic idea)
The Son of God (a different species of being)
The Good Shepherd (one who cares)
Counsellor (source of wisdom)
The Prince of Peace (reconciler)

These are names given to him by others or, in the canonical tradition, by himself. Thus, his role as hero has always been represented in the names by which he has been called. I have a name for him too. For me, he is the "Man of Light."

On a wall in our house, there is a picture of Jesus laughing. I love it, and I imagine what this Jesus is like. Clearly, he has a wonderful sense of humor. As an alive, sensitive, perceptive human being, he sees the ridiculous as well as the sublime. He loves a good joke. He revels in the beautiful gifts he has received as a human being, living his life in the flesh. He seems to tell me that I need to learn to laugh with a profound gratitude when I receive each new gift from God's hand—my family each day, my friends each day, my lover each day, my hope, my mind, my creativity, and always, moment by moment, the reality of my life in God.

So we need a hero, one who recognizes the inconsistencies in our own human behavior. He is one who knows how powerful the negative forces are in our spirits, as well as the positive and creative peacemaking forces there. So he is patient with us—his sisters and brothers. And by his patient love for all, he tells us that this is the way the Great Spirit, who is God, views us and treats us as well. Instead of becoming angry with our stupidity, he smiles. Instead of lashing out at our inhumanity to others, he reaches out his arms and pulls us to his breast. He shakes his head and there are tears in those laughing eyes, and we are shamed by his patience and healed by his love.

That is what I need and so do you.

We need a hero—one to whom we can look. No theologian's doctrine of God is sufficient, and certainly not mine. No theory, no fact, is good enough. We need to see it somehow.

We need to see a prototype of what it is to be human, what it is to be faithful, what it is to love our neighbor, what it is to be patient, what it is to be generous, what it is to exercise self-control, and what it is to live in harmony with God. We need to see our own possibilities made manifest in the flesh. We need to see what it looks like to receive the gifts of our humanity, our intelligence, our creativity, our sexuality, our power of speech. That is why we need a hero.

If Jesus is our hero, he is also our ideal. He is the pioneer of our faith, for he has gone before. He has discovered he is in God, and God is in him. He has come to us to bring his blessings, his revelations, and his power to love and endure. We need to hear his teachings. What he has to say and show us about our relationships with other people. How we can exercise compassion and mercy. How we can discipline ourselves to allow God to impact our own spirits always more and more deeply.

Yes, we also need to learn from him how to weep when our fellow human beings weep and cry out and suffer—when disease wracks their bodies, when hostility alienates them from their fellows, when weariness of life threatens their peace, when loss rips them apart. And with our tears, we need to dress their wounds.

This will be the one whom we can hold before our minds. Our hero and our ideal, the one who has pioneered the life of faith and come out on top. The mythical Jesus must be a story out of which one may live his life, but it can be that only if it responds effectively to the fundamental universal needs of the human spirit.

The next chapter, therefore, tells the mythic tale of my hero, the "Man of Light."[82]

Chapter 6

✦

The Man of Light—a Mythic Tale

The Beginning

At some lost, hidden time, the world of spirit spoke, made stone and
leaf, made flesh, took shape,
and change was born.

And so the world of stormy nature had issued from the loins of God.

Then leaped from out the womb of God, a myriad sparks of self, new
spirits joined
to one another, offspring of God's womb.

Every spirit donned a cloak of flesh, animating bodies sprung from
God's imagination.

Each infant spirit, with the genes of God, became a child in the storm
within, behind which
lurked the Spirit who is God.

And thus they lived, storm battered, rain blinded, wind whipped, until
there came the one
who was to come in lightning's flash.

The Coming

A man named Jesus, soul and body, came walking on the earth, a
wanderer seeking vision.

And all his search for meaning came up nothing worth.

He perused the libraries of great cities, walked the shores of pristine
lakes, tasted labor's sweat,
and wandered halls of royalty—and all was vanity.

He walked through raging night and no light showed his way.
The wind whipped through the trees as though to tear them from their
roots, and tumbled rolling
clouds across the sky.
Rain lashed his face as if to shred his skin, and no star winked at him
to say it's all a joke and morning will reveal the calm of day.
He walked through raging night, as darkness stole his sight.

And then, the lightning flashed—a single bolt of light leaped from out
the clouds and
somewhere struck the earth!
For one split second everything was stopped and all was very bright.
The whipping branches fixed and still.
The rolling clouds had ceased their flight.
The driving sheets of rain were halt.
And thus he glimpsed beyond the wildness of the night as all the
countryside was frozen
in a flash of light.
He glimpsed the real behind the storm, a world at peace, a world that
did not break, and did not stumble.
It was an intimation of another world yet somehow intermeshed, not
separated from the storm.
A world of spirit and of grace, a world of beauty and of peace.
So in his soul the storm was stilled. The wind had ceased to blow, the
rain fell gently,
a great light shone, and the hidden face of God came clear.
Battered, beaten by the storm he cried out to the light,
"Show me the way!"

The Vision

Then, from the light of lightning's flash, a voice called out his name.
And the light about him was the light of understanding.

The voice said: "I am all about you like the light. You live in me, my
light in you.
In every living soul, my light's a single ray for each one lives in me, like
you do too.

81

But they don't know their soul's own light is also mine.
The darkness in their souls assails their light to make all dark within.
But I will not allow my light to die."

The voice of God said: "I am also in the storm, behind and through it
just 'cause you
are there as well.
When you contend, then I contend, for you are part of me.
When you are hurt, then I do hurt, for you are part of me.
Your joy is my joy, your pleasure mine.
Because your spirit lives in human flesh, then I do live there too."
And Jesus asked the light:
"What must I do?"

The voice's light said: "You must let your light blaze forth.
My gifts of spirit gratefully receive, enjoy, improve, and use for love.
I give you intellect and creativity, the power to decide and act, but just
to use for love.
My gifts of flesh receive, to thank for and enjoy, improve, and use for
love.
I give you strength, endurance, sexuality, and all the senses, all to use
for love.
You must teach to look for me within themselves.
You must teach the way of light, so they can drive away their dark and
make all light within.
Together we shall bring in peace, for I will shine my face on them as I
have shined my face on you.
The light of my face shall bring my healing.
The storms will still, my light will be as oil upon their heads and joy
within their hearts.
And you will be the light among them. You will teach them and they
will hear."

So then the light of lightning fled away, but the light in his soul grew
bright and he walked
with step as sure as light.

The Message

Among the least and greatest, Jesus came awalking.

In him, God's peace now reigned.

In him, all power-of-no lay prone, all power-of-yes stood tall.

So thus, with laughter 'fore the storm he came, his spirit still as the
Spirit who is God is still.

Outside the storm raged on, and all the souls, struck like sparks from
out the womb of God did gaze on him.

And who saw they?

They saw the one who merits honor, stirs imagination, who wakes their
vision
to the possibilities of life.

And what heard they?

They heard him weep.

He wept to feel another's pain.

He wept to see the greedy steal.

Whene'er injustice checked fair play, whene'er self-righteousness divided
souls apart,
whene'er the pious killed for pride—he wept.

He wept.

What else heard they?

They heard him laugh.

He laughed at all the petty stuff.

He laughed at slights and slanders, at the pomp of prideful ones.

He laughed when beauty moved him, and when love had pleasured
him, whene'er he saw
the mercy of forgiveness

He laughed with holy joy when foes were reconciled, when rival faiths
embraced, and when he saw the peace and joy of others.

He laughed with great guffaw at threat of death.

To them he said, "If one has all this life has promised, but yet
extinguishes the light of hope,
he loses.

If one has lived the life indulgent and of privilege, but scorns the life
of spirit, then his light

fades fast away.
You must not fear the ones who whip or curse or kill the flesh.
But rather, pity sadly those who want to snuff your light, because your
  spirit cannot die,
    for it's a flame in God's great fire."

He's the man who modeled pow'r to vanquish fear.
To love without a hesitation.
To stand unmoved against injustice.
To show compassion unencumbered.
T"is the one who taught to go the second mile.
To turn the other cheek,
To wield nor sword nor voice in anger.
He taught their light could brighter burn and fill up all their life, and
  they would find that by that light, they all were linked to one
  another.
He taught the light that shone in every sympathetic word, in every act
  of mercy,
    and in works of healing, was the light that was the reign of God.

He taught to laugh with sheer delight at all the beauties of the flesh,
  the happiness of friendship,
    and the joy of love.
He taught to trust at last the night would be alight.
Each act of healing, deed of blessing Jesus wrought was bathed in
  light.
He demonstrated spirit's pow'r o'er nature and o'er storm, o'er ills of
  mind and body,
    o'er the violence of nations
His power was the power to fill each soul with light
    that was the light in him.

The Going

But those in whom the dark was darker than their light was bright
   didn't understand.
His way the way of peace, but his brothers and his sisters did not covet
   peace.
His way the way of self-effacing love but all such love was seen as
   weakness.
His way led through the storm into the life of spirit, but they were
   blinded by the wind
   and by the rain.
Their leaders feared his strange advice would rob them of their power.
They feared the people who believed in him would cease to heed
   them.
To love their enemies did not made sense to them.
To turn the other cheek, it ran from all they had been taught.
They did not see the light that shone in him, around him.
They did not recognize the healing power of that light.

For reasons such as these the hero of our life was threatened.
They threatened him with prison — he went on shining light and
   laughing at their foolishness.
They threatened him with firing squad — he laughed at all their show
   of power and authority.
He knew the light was in him and he was unafraid.
At last, they chose to cast him out and be forever rid of his insanity.
So he was exiled to a distant land, but he went there laughing, laughing
   all the way!

The Return

And still the story does not end.
He laughed because he'd seen the glory on the face of God.
He laughed because he knew the power of his spirit.
The light went with him and surrounded him, even as he planned his
   sure return.
Three days passed.
And then he landed on the shore from which he'd sailed away.
Where the storm still raged, he came victorious.

So now we know that spirit, which was his, is ours as well and we can
   also rise from out
   the midst of storm to weep, to laugh, to love.

Again he walks among the least, the greatest.
The light still blazes from within and burns yet brighter than before.
And now he lives for us, our hero and ideal, and walks among us full
   of light.
And that light is the Light of God.

Chapter 7

✦

Jesus for Today

How can this Man of Light live for us today?

Well, every period in Western history has produced its own predominant picture of Jesus. Only the first of them is closely based on knowledge of the peasant figure known to have once walked, taught, and died in Roman Palestine.

In every period, three criteria had to be met in order to bring Jesus alive for that age. First, it had to take off from some inherited tradition about Jesus, from spoken remembrances to begin with, and eventually from scripture. Second, it needed to employ the unique expectations of the culture, its world view and its lifestyles, and its changing scientific, theological, and political exigencies. Third, at least some of the universal needs of the human species had to be met. These three factors converged to form the dominant image of the Jesus honored and projected by each historical period.

However, our own time demands something new. It cries out for authenticity and reality in a way never experienced before. Pomposity, royal authority, or esoteric, secret knowledge are highly suspect. We are not ready to accept our beliefs just because somebody presumed to say they were so. Therefore, our times require of our image of Jesus that it must somehow make rational sense, however mythical, and that it reflect our present world view, philosophical or scientific. And, as in any age, it must serve to meet at least some of the universal human needs shared by all the members of the human species.

These needs are universal because they do not change from culture to culture. Cultural changes, as well as political and theological influences, neither create, remove, nor modify them. They belong to the human species by reason of the nature of the human spirit. They reside at the center of the basic human experience. In some way, each living image of Jesus has at least partially met some of the universal needs for that time.

There are, naturally, a finite number of universal human needs, but I am under no illusion that I have identified them all. There are five, however, which I have come to believe are basic.

Only if the image of Jesus I have suggested is rationally believable and able to meet these five needs in some significant measure, do I dare to hope it can serve my spiritual life or that of anyone living in the twenty-first century. So, in this final chapter, I want to point out how the story of the Man of Light can meet those universal needs.

The Man of Light Gives Us Hope

No human being can exist long without hope. Hope may be variously defined, but I am thinking about the reality of a hope that remains when all other petty, temporary hopes are shattered. Our temporal hopes can sustain us for a while, perhaps only from day to day. Sometimes that is all that gets us through. But if that primordial hope fades, the light of life goes out.

One of the great dramas of the so-called theater of the absurd was *Waiting for Godot* by Samuel Beckett. Now revived on Broadway, it has four characters who are waiting for someone called Godot to show up. But he never does. So what is the play all about? Seasoned actors playing the roles have always struggled to make out what Beckett was trying to say. Those who are currently doing the play on Broadway also struggle, but they have finally decided that it is simply about the life that every human being experiences. Life appears to be without meaning. So we are reduced to the effort to endure, that is, to wait for—whatever. In the play, a number of alternatives to waiting are contemplated, suicide among them. But none is chosen and so they wait; they endure. Why? Because someone is coming; hope still flickers. And there ends the play.

In our hero, the flicker of hope remained in the midst of the storm. That is what enabled him to search and cry out in his despair. And the Light revealed itself and spoke to him. But the Light awaited the moment to flash when, in humility and out of that elemental hope, he cried out.

I look in vain for the right word to characterize this hope, for I'm not talking about the makeshift hopes that prop us up, but the presence of a tiny light that will not go out.

In our hero, we see the human spirit in its native state as alienated and lost from the reality of his life. Still, we see him bearing in his own spirit, not oblivion, but a glimmering hope, an awareness of his alienated self and his longing for orientation and focus. We see there the potential that resides in every human, a readiness for some small flame to blaze and a humility that cries out. It is the pervasive light that glows within us as human beings until we come to understand our inescapable and indestructible connection with the Light, which is God.

So, when we look on our hero, we see that glimmer of hope in the darkness of the storm and we know that same hope is also ours. If it grows dim, we cry out again. But always we feed on that inexhaustible supply. And because it is always there, we may hope in the Greater Light, in the fullness of the possibilities of our own humanity, even as we see them fulfilled in our hero, our ideal.

This is a hope that says there is a future, no matter what. It is an uncertain future. Its content is yet unknown. But without it, the spirit enters hell. Dante drew his picture of the gates of hell, over which the following words were inscribed, "Abandon hope, all who enter here."[83]

Hope may be the greatest of the needs of the human spirit. Or perhaps they cannot be ordered at all.

The Man of Light Gives Us Connection

I take Jesus, my mythic hero, to be the prototype of humanness.

So this hero of our life manifests an indestructible hope in the midst of his despair—a receptivity to a light he cannot see. It is a light not separate from the storms of his natural life, but it flashes through the storm and fills him with a light he had not known before. He is no different from any other human creature, for the light belongs to each, and each is a part of the Greater Light. Thus, as the bearer of the Light which is God, he is inseparably connected to every other spirit in whom that light shines.

In this image of Jesus, the pervasiveness of God is symbolized by the light. Because all possess light, however weak the flicker, we each are part of the light of God who is all Light. So, God is in each of us in some degree or other. In reality we are never alone, for we are always connected to one another in God. Thus, our prayers for one another all go through God.

This speaks to me because in a hundred ways through my already-long life, I have been aware I was alone—that no one else experienced what I experienced, had my thoughts, or felt my emotions. No one could really know me in the way that I know me. I longed for a more intimate connection. Nearly everything I did seemed to be a reaching out for something that was missing. Maybe for someone. Maybe for some community of persons. Maybe for some place where I felt like I belonged—like I was at home. But all it did was to help me forget, for a while, that I still felt alone.

When we see this connection, we understand that we can never stand or walk alone, for the light in us is but a flame in the Light that is God. We hear what the Light says to our hero and what he is sent to teach his brothers and sisters, and we understand that every connection we cultivate, from the most casual act of cooperation to the profoundest act of love, is a sacramental connection that enhances the reality of our spiritual connection to the Light who is God.

And we can believe it, not because our hero says it, but because when he speaks, he speaks as another human being of what we also now begin to experience in our own self-awareness. In this twenty-first century, we are no longer ready to accept things of a deeply personal nature on authority alone. We are not ready to believe any longer in the old puppeteer in the sky. But the God who is "the light that enlightens every man that comes into the world" is a God who makes sense both intellectually, and also in terms of our personal experience.

When we see our hero connected to everyone else because everyone else is spirit just like we are, then the possibility of our connecting with others is laid upon us like a promise. And the reality of our connection with every other spirit is realized in us as we contemplate the hero of our life.

So why does our hero laugh with us at our frailty and our failures and not condemn us? Because he, our ideal human being, loves us and the connection is affirmed, sealed, and guaranteed. Is he satisfied with

90

us? No, no! He just wants to help us become what we can become—complete human beings, like he is.

Because each of us is an individual, the universal human need for connection may be at least as important as our need for hope.

The Man of Light Gives Us Meaning

It is abundantly clear from the immense popularity of Rick Warren's recent book, *The Purpose Driven Life,* that there is a hunger for the meaning of human existence. But is it universal? I strongly believe it is. Warren's book is but a symptom.

In the West, the mislabeled "happiness" thesis of Aristotle has often served as an explanation for all human action. While not an accurate representation of Aristotle's "eudaemonism," it claims everyone acts always in the interests of his own happiness. Therefore, the purpose of life is to find happiness.

A major philosophical position known as "hedonism" affirms that the expectation of pleasure drives all our decisions, and thus pleasure is the meaning of life. But both of these theories are actually theories of action and do not deal with our search for meaning.

Our need for meaning is not for a theory about why we do what we do. Rather, it is a profoundly human experience that seems to arise out of our contentless hope. Hope itself cries out for a recognizable focus. Or, to put it in other words, *hope* is focused on the future, either long-term or short-term, but *meaning* refers to the need for fulfillment in the present. Meaning is found in the doing; that is, in the process, rather than in the assurance that there is a future.

Therefore, we remember that our hero received a mandate from the Light. Out of the vision of the Light, of which his own light was a part, and the understanding that every human spirit shared in that same light, the meaning of his own life was born. The purpose of his life became that of embodying in himself a shining flame of the Greater Light, and bearing witness to what it meant to live in that Light and become a bearer of that Light. Thus, the meaning of his life was given him and his hope became focused.

One of the sayings attributed to Jesus in the canon was a question: "What does it profit a man if he gain the whole world and lose his own soul?" The answer to that is clear—it profits him nothing. The meaning of life, as we see it in our heroic story of Jesus, is that he was saving his own soul. He was treating himself as a sacred part of God to whom all is owed. And he treated everyone else as sacred parts of God. He used all his positive gifts in the service of others and, thus, saved his own soul. And he taught that that was what worked. The meaning of his life was the doing, the teaching, and the healing.

Is this a purpose sufficient for our lives? I can only tell you that when I hold up my hero, my ideal, this Man of Light, I find there is no other meaning that so draws me and so fills my soul.

This, of course, says nothing about what career, or vocation, or labor one may choose, or that may choose one. But it says everything about our stewardship of all our gifts and relationships. And it is a meaning that cannot be destroyed by vicissitudes or setbacks, for it is given to us by the Light that can never go out.

The Man of Light Gives Us Guidance

But finding the meaning or purpose of one's life is not enough, for it immediately begins to introduce technical questions about "how?" If we take the meaning of our life, its purpose, to be and shine the Light, then we need to discover how to exercise our stewardship of the Light.

The first part of the answer is given by our circumstances. That is, where and when do we live? What limits of time, space, and gifts have we inherited? What opportunities do our circumstances afford us?

How do we live this meaning? How do we rise each morning and use the hours before us? How can we apply the purpose of our life to our means of livelihood? What about this family, this wife or husband, the children and grandchildren whom we have had a share in creating? How can we form our relationships with these who are precious to us?

And if we learn from our hero to laugh with gratitude over the gifts we have received, then how shall we love this life we've been given, love the body we have, the family we've made, the society in which we live, and the human community of which we are inescapably a part?

Even more puzzling, what about our avocations, our recreation, our hobbies, and even the whole world of sport? And how do we express the meaning of our life in the arts?

Finding the answers sounds like an impossible task, doesn't it? But we still have our hero, our ideal. Nebulous, fanciful, unreal? No! He is real in the sense that we hold this picture of him in our mind and heart, this ideal of what it truly means to be fully human—what it truly means to be divine.

The gifts we are thankful for and revel in must remain gifts; they may not be allowed to occupy the place of our life's meaning, lest we lose our souls. Such gifts are the pleasures of life, the successes, the glory, and the good reputation. In our hero and ideal, we see that we may lose all these things, but we will gain everything if the meaning of our lives is to blow upon the embers of light within us so as to grow our own soul and manifest the Light of God.

So we have no right to despise our blessings or cease to take pleasure in them, but we will give thanks for them, cultivate them, enjoy them, and use them in whatever ways we can to shed the Light.

Therefore, when we look to Jesus, our ideal human, we hear him speak his wisdom about the deeds which produce unity, harmony, healing, and peace—going the second mile, turning the other cheek, lifting up neither sword nor voice in anger, loving without reservation, standing firm against injustice, and meting out compassion without conditions. We see that the Light that shines in every deed of compassion, in every act of mercy, and work of healing is, in fact, the Light that is God.

Again, when we listen to Jesus, we hear him weep when it is time to weep and hear him laugh when it is time to laugh. He guides our struggle to become more and more human, more and more divine.

The Man of Light Gives Us Understanding

Finally, the need to understand is also universal among human beings. We are not only self-aware, but we are aware of that which is not our self. At a very early age, humans learn that the toes they discover nearby are really a part of their own body, but the blanket covering them is not. When they find themselves trusting someone who is not themselves, they become curious to learn about the one whom they trust—the object of their faith. Thus, the person of faith must also ask what it is he trusts, what it is he fears, and why. In fact, centuries ago, Aristotle noted that the search for understanding begins with the experience of awe.

We need to understand what we hope for, what we are connected to and not identical with, the object of our love and our passion, the meaning of life, and what is really important in life. We need to be able to organize these things in our mind—to think about and discuss these things. Unless we attain some level of understanding, we can neither anticipate the consequences of our actions, nor weigh the values involved in possible actions. We can neither decide, nor act, on our decisions.

There are some people who seem to care little about understanding, but that is not because they do not want to understand. Rather, they do not want to have their current understandings questioned or exert themselves to wrestle with issues—political, social, or religious— about which they have already made up their minds. They have their understandings or assumptions. They simply do not want to exert themselves to answer objections or listen to alternatives. But they need some kind of understanding to function at all.

So, if we hold our hero in our hearts and allow this image of our ideal human to inform our minds, then we are given an understanding of many things. We understand that God is like the sun—wherever sunlight is found, there is the sun. Just so, wherever light is found, there is God—the Greater Light. We understand that in every human being there is, at least, the light of a primordial hope. We understand the light within may be fanned into a flame that burns with a great passion. We understand that our light is a part of the Greater Light who is God. We understand that every light in every human breast is but one more flame that burns alongside our flames in the Greater Light who is God. We come to understand that we are connected, therefore, to every other person because every other person is also connected to God—the Greater Light. We understand that that connection is permanent and cannot be broken. We are given an understanding of the meaning of our lives and our responsibility as bearers of the light. Hope is born in us, and the seeds of a holy love are planted.

We understand that to take this mythic image of Jesus as our hero and ideal is an aid and a benefit in our lifelong struggle to harmonize our spirits with that of the Head of the Spirit world "in whom we live, move, and have our being."[84] But he meets our needs in something more than a rational way. It's not a sentimental journey, but our emotions brilliantly color it, and our way is lighted.

Let me remind you again that we cannot believe Jesus did everything the writings, canonical and apocryphal, say he did. We cannot believe all they tell us he said. We have to be realistic about what the New Testament is, and we have to understand that it is not history. As Bart Ehrman makes clear, history is confined to those facts for which there is compelling evidence. And I have gone as far as history will take me.

Therefore, I asked what options I now had before me. One, I could simply forget Jesus. Two, I could try, somehow, like Schweitzer, to appropriate the "spirit" of the traditions about him. Three, I could create an image of Jesus that does not depend on historical evidence, though it builds loosely upon those few historical facts the scholars have established and boldly uses the Q material as the best approximation of his actual teachings. I have chosen the third option.

Therefore, my picture of Jesus does not depend on historical evidence, though it does build loosely upon those few historical facts that scholars have established. It also boldly uses the Q material as the best approximation of his actual teachings. Like everyone else, I have brought my imagination to bear upon those facts. I have not dared to allow it to run wild, but have directed it to serve those universal needs which I perceive every human being possesses by reason of his being human. That is to say, I have attempted to create an image of Jesus which can speak to those needs.

Again, that is exactly what both the Gnostic church and its enemy, the orthodox Gentile church, attempted to do. That is also what Christians throughout the centuries have done. They all created a Jesus to meet their own perceived needs. In doing so, some of their universal needs were also met.

For me, Jesus, this Man of Light, is the banner I fly—the touchstone by which I judge myself. He is the sign by which I know who I am. He is the beauty of holiness, the lily of the valley. He is the promise of my future, the bright and morning star. He is the ideal I hold before my eyes, the hero I honor and applaud.

I recommend him to you for your blessing and joy.

Finally, Think on These Things!

- We don't have to worry anymore about finding the historical Jesus. We never will.
- We don't have to proclaim him as the one and only savior of the world. He isn't.
- We can have a more satisfying perspective on suffering in the world. We can both weep and laugh.
- We can assume our own responsibilities instead of laying everything on the kind of God whom we now know doesn't exist.
- We need not be haunted by the suspicion that we are living a lie. Now God who is Spirit begins to make sense.
- We can be more comfortable relating to people who are seekers just as we are. We don't have to have an answer for every question.
- We don't ever have to be alone again. Not only do we live, move and have our being in God, but we are also inseparably and eternally connected with every spirit who ever lived.
- We may always choose to look to Jesus, our hero and ideal, our model of what it means to be fully human and, therefore, fully divine.
- And finally, we may look forward to another chance at the perfecting of our spirits in love, peace, and joy when they are at last set free.

Appendix A
A Jesus Timeline

Third Isaiah (56-66)	(post-Exile promises)	
Jeremiah	(post-Exile promises)	
Plato	(used in adaptation to Roman culture)	427–347 BCE
Aristotle	(used in adaptation to Roman culture)	384–322 BCE
Origin of Apocalyptic	(means revelation of future)	225 BCE
Maccabean Revolt		167–164 BCE
Birth of Jesus		7–4 BCE
Death of Jesus		26–29 CE
The Sayings Gospel Q	(perhaps in Syria)	50–60 CE
Paul's seven letters		50–60 CE
1 Thessalonians	(from Corinth)	50–51 CE
1 Corinthians	(from Ephesus)	53–54 CE
Philippians	(from prison in Ephesus)	55–56CE
Philemon	(from prison in Ephesus)	55–56 CE
Galatians	(from Ephesus)	55–57 CE
2 Corinthians	(two or more stages, from Ephesus and Philippi)	55-56 CE
Romans	(from Corinth)	58 CE

Paul visits James in Jerusalem	(start of split)	50 CE
Collection delivered by Paul to Jerusalem church		59 CE
Epictetus	(Roman writer)	60–130 CE
Execution of James, brother of Jesus		61 CE
Death of Paul and Peter in Rome		62–64 CE
Rise of Gnosticism		during the split
Great fire in Rome		64 CE
Destruction of Temple and Jerusalem		70 CE

Nag Hammadi discoveries (fifty-three mostly Gnostic documents discovered in 1945 CE), written during the second half of first century through fourth century
> Examples:
> Gospel of Thomas (influenced by Docetism, perhaps Gnosticism as well) 60–70 CE
> Gospel of Philip
> Apocryphon of John
> Gospel of Truth
> Gospel to the Egyptians
> Secret Book of James
> Apocalypse of Paul
> Letter of Peter to Philip
> Apocalypse of Peter
> Gospel of Mary Magdalene
> Treatise on Resurrection

Rabbinic movement	(Reaction to fall of Jerusalem and the Temple)	70 CE ff
Ebionites	(Jewish Christians reject Rabbinic movement)	70 CE ff
Gospel of Mark	(Gentile response to destruction of the Temple)	70-75 CE
Gospel of Matthew	(Jewish struggle with Pharisees, upper Galilee)	80–90 CE
Gospel of the Nazareans	(Jewish Christian audience)	80–90 CE
Gospel of Luke and Acts of the Apostles	(Christian self-definition)	90–110 CE
Josephus	(non-Christian source)	95 CE
Gospel of John and The Revelation of John	(for Gentiles living in Rome))	95—120 CE
Split with Judaism completed		100 CE
Ignatius, Bishop in Antioch	(fought Docetism)	ca. 115 CE
Polycarp, Bishop in Smyrna	(fought Docetism))	ca. 115 CE
Letter to the Hebrews		100–120 CE
Tertullian	(heresy hunter turned Montanist)	110 CE
Shepherd of Hermas	(focus on character)	110–140 CE
Tacitus	(Roman source on Christian movement)	wrote in 117 CE

1 John	(with John, seeks to reconcile Docetism with crucifixion)	120–130 CE
Marcus Aurelius	(enemy of Gnosticism and a martyr)	121–180 CE
Justin	(apologist; doctrinal basis of orthodoxy)	100–160 CE
Barnabas	(first to propose idea of Christian scripture)	131 CE
Bar Kochba Revolt	(second rebellion)	133–135 CE
Marcion	(his list excluded the Hebrew scriptures)	excommunicated in 144 CE
Montanus	(father of Montanism)	appeared in 156 CE
Irenaeus	(wrote against heresies, defined orthodoxy)	185 CE
Clement of Alexandria	(Platonist Christian)	died in 215 CE
Origen	(first systematic theologian, Platonist)	182–254 CE
Muratorian Canon	(first appearance of the list of books in the New Testament)	ca. 200 CE
First use of "Catholic" to exclude heretics		end of second century
Plotinus	(neo-Platonist)	205–220 CE
Hippolytus	(wrote against heresies)	ca. 230 CE
Eusebius, Bishop in Caesaria	(wrote church history)	310–324 CE
Athanasius	(Jesus both human and divine)	296–373 CE

Arias	(Jesus midway between human and divine)	325 CE
Council of Nicea	(Incarnation formalized)	325 CE
Council of Constantinople	(Trinity formalized)	381 CE
Council of Carthage	(New Testament canon adopted)	394 CE
Church architecture began to develop		350–400 CE
Apostles' Creed	(derived from baptismal formula)	dates from 400 CE
Rise of biblical scholarship		Seventeenth Century
Jefferson Bible	(early effort to sort out Jesus' sayings)	1821
Schweitzer's *"Quest"*	(key to modern scholarly search for historical Jesus)	1906
Nag Hammadi documents discovered		1945
Dead Sea Scrolls discovered		beginning in 1947
Jesus' tomb theory	(Jesus intended to establish a political dynasty)	Tomb discovered in 2000
Gospel of Judas finally translated	(has Judas conspiring with Jesus to betray him)	2000 CE

Appendix B
A Homily—My Man, Jesus

Comment

There may be those who, having read the chapters of this book, will think the foundations of the Christian faith have been destroyed. However, I reject this assumption. To be sure, the foundations of Christian orthodoxy, which are already in the process of crumbling, have been attacked, not Christian faith. But the Gospel of Jesus, as taken from the teachings in the Q material, remains and can become the new foundation of a Jesus movement whose shape is not yet clearly discernible.

The following homily is intended to demonstrate one way the Gospel of Jesus can speak profoundly to the universal needs of the human spirit.

My Man, Jesus

A child cries out in the night. There is a storm raging. The wind is blowing. The rain is falling. Then a flash of lightening splits the night sky. A sudden crash of thunder shakes the windows and the child cries out in terror!

His mother comes and sits by his side on the bed. She tries to console her little boy who is still sobbing. She says, "Don't be afraid. God is right here with you. He'll protect you."

But the boy says, "I know, Mommie, but I can't see him. How can he protect me? I just want you to protect me. I want you to talk to me."

Well, there is a little child like that in all of us. We'd like to see God too. It would help if we could see him and hear his voice and feel his arms around us like those of our mommie's.

Or again, here is a young woman whose heart is torn in two. Her husband has walked out on her and left her with three little children to provide for and rear. Her pastor comes to visit her, and he tells her to trust God because God will provide. Then he prays with her and, she thanks him.

But when he's gone, she breaks down and sobs her heart out. She tries to pray. She says, "Dear God, help me, help me, help me! Where are you, God? I can't see you. I can't touch you. I can't hear you. How can you help me?"

Now, let me ask you, what kind of God is this who can't be seen, or touched, or heard? He's so far away!

"Well, you just have to believe," someone tells me. Mothers and pastors and friends are usually ready to fall back on blind faith because there seems to be no firm reality available.

All the claims that God protected my son from the bullets of war or that he healed my wife of her cancer are simply quashed by the quiet observation that he didn't protect the other three or four thousand young men and women from the violence in Iraq, or the millions of men, women, and children who have died of cancer.

So where has he been? Where is he now? Millions and millions of prayers are sent up every day of the year from all around the earth. And millions of those prayers, maybe most of those prayers, have received no visible, concrete answer. Is he deaf? Is he blind? Has he no heart, no sympathy, no compassion?

I need something more than blind belief. I need something more than a book to make God real to me. I need something more than a king or a bishop or a preacher to tell me what I should believe. I need to understand how it can be that God exists and cares and is closer than my hands and my feet.

What I'm getting at is this—the reality of God cannot be found through some proof that God exists. The reality of God cannot be found through some emotional experience of what we call "conversion" or being "born again." For emotions ebb and flow and are totally undependable. They prove nothing. They guarantee nothing.

You see, he is not someone who has been hidden and must be found. He is not someone who is so far away that we can't know where he is. He is not someone so impossible that he defies belief. He does not have to be found. He does not have to be found because we already experience him every day of our lives

We just need someone to point him out to us, to show us how he loves us. We need someone whom we can see and hear and feel, who can touch us and speak to us and hold us close, in whom we can see what God is doing.

We need someone—like Jesus maybe?

But all we really know for certain about the real Jesus—that is, with historically certifiable knowledge—is that, once upon a time, he was a Jewish peasant who walked the dusty roads of Palestine, taught about the Kingdom of God, and was crucified on a Roman cross. That's about it. Nothing more with any certainty.

What we need is someone we can see and hear and feel now, not in history, but in this very moment. So I want to share with you the Jesus I hold in my heart, for it is there, in my heart, that I can see and hear and feel him. There it is that he shows me how God provides for our deepest needs.

On a wall in our house there is a picture of Jesus laughing. I love it, and I imagine what this Jesus is like. Clearly, he has a wonderful sense of humor. As an alive, sensitive, perceptive human being, he sees the ridiculous as well as the sublime. He loves a good joke, and he revels in the beautiful gifts he has received as a human being living his life in the flesh.

He tells me that I need to learn to laugh with a profound gratitude when I receive each new gift from God's hand—my life each day, my friends each day, my lover each day, my hope, my mind, my creativity, and always, moment by moment, the reality of my life in God.

He recognizes the inconsistencies in our human behavior. He knows how powerful the negative forces are, as well as the positive and creative peacemaking forces there—he knows them, for he knows all these things in himself. So he is patient with us—his sisters and his brothers. And by his patient love for all of us, he tells us that's the way the Great Spirit who is God in us views us—and treats us as well.

Instead of becoming angry with our stupidity, he smiles. Instead of lashing out at our inhumanity to others, he reaches out his arms and pulls us to his breast. He shakes his head and there are tears in those laughing eyes, and we are shamed by his patience and healed by his love.

That is what I need and I believe you do too. I need a hero—one to whom I can look. No theologian's doctrine of God is sufficient, and certainly not mine. No theory, no creed is good enough. I need to see it somehow.

I need to see a prototype of what it is to be human, what it is to be faithful, what it is to love my neighbor, what it is to be patient, what it is to be generous, what it is to exercise self-control, and what it is to live in harmony with God. I need to see my own possibilities made manifest in the flesh. I need to see what it looks like to receive the gifts of my humanity, my intelligence, my creativity, my sexuality, my power of speech.

I need to hear his teachings—what he has to say and show me about my relationships with other people. How I can exercise compassion and mercy. How I can discipline myself to allow God to impact my own spirit always more and more deeply.

He has come to us to bring his blessings, his revelations, and his power to laugh and to love.

I also need to learn from him how to weep when my fellow human beings weep, and cry out, and suffer—when disease wracks their bodies, when hostility alienates them from their fellows, when weariness of life threatens their peace, when loss rips them apart. And with my tears, I need to dress their wounds as God weeps and, with his tears, dresses mine.

He provides our deepest needs—not, most certainly, all our wants, but, most certainly, all our deepest needs. This Jesus is the one whom I hold in my heart—my hero and my ideal.

He is also the one who protects me from all fear. He's the one who has pioneered the life of faith and come out on top. He has been disappointed, rebuffed, scorned, unjustly accused, beaten, and even murdered. And he has born it all without complaint. For this was the world into which he was placed in order to manifest to us the power of the human spirit to endure, to survive, to live without surrender—and more than that—to live victoriously!

The Jesus story must be a story from which one may live his life. When he speaks, we listen. Not because he's some messenger from another world, but because he speaks as another human being, of what we also now begin to experience in our own self-awareness as human beings.

In this twenty-first century we can know the God who is "the light that enlightens every man and woman who comes into the world" because we see the light at work in our hero and our ideal—in our Jesus.

He protects us from all our fears because he manifests the spirit that endures and survives. He himself faced down every fear that assailed him. He protects us because he shows us that every human being has the courage to confront all the obstacles that life puts in the way of his happiness, and the strength to refuse to allow them to destroy him.

He provides for us because he demonstrates that the human spirit can decide to be happy no matter what. Because he is human just like we are, we can do it too! I know this not just because he demonstrated it, but because I have known other persons who have done precisely this.

One of the questions Jesus is said to have asked was, "What does it profit a man if he gain the whole world and lose his own soul?" The answer to that is clear—it profits him nothing. The meaning of life, as we see it in the heroic story of Jesus, is that he was saving his own soul. He was treating himself as a sacred part of God to whom all is owed, and he treated everyone else as sacred parts of God. He taught that that was what worked. The meaning of his life was the doing, the teaching, and the healing. In other words, the bearing of the Light.

Is this a purpose sufficient for my life? When I gaze upon my hero, my ideal, my Jesus, I find there is no other meaning that so draws me and so fills me. It is a meaning that cannot be destroyed by vicissitudes or setbacks, for it is given to us by the Light that can never go out.

So, if I hold my hero in my heart and allow this image of my ideal human being to inform my mind, then I am also given an understanding of many things.

Then I understand that God is like the sun—wherever sunlight is found, there is the sun. Just so, wherever light is found, there is God—the Greater Light.

I understand that in every human being there is at least the light of a primordial hope.

I understand the light within may be fanned into a flame that burns with a great passion.

I understand that my light is a part of the Greater Light who is God.

I understand every light in every human breast is but one more flame that burns alongside my flame in the Greater Light who is God.

I come to understand that I am connected, therefore, to every other person because every other person is also connected to God, the Greater Light.

I understand that that connection is permanent and cannot be broken.

I am given an understanding of the meaning of my life and my responsibility as a bearer of the Light. Hope is born in me and the seeds of a holy love are planted.

I understand that to take this Jesus as my hero and ideal is an aid and a benefit in my lifelong struggle to harmonize my spirit with that of the Head of the Spirit world "in whom I live, move, and have my being."

God does not have to be found because we already experience him every day. We just need someone to point him out to us. Therefore, we need not fear, for there is nothing in heaven or on earth that can separate us from the God in whom we live and who lives in us.

So be it. Amen.

Notes

All quotations from the Bible are taken from the New International Version. All quotations from Jamrs M. Robinson's translation of the "Sayings Gospel Q" appear in his *The Gospel of Jesus*. See note 41. Their references in the text identify their locations in the Bible and in *Thomas*.

Note to the Introduction: Who Was Jesus Really?

1. James D. Tabor, *The Jesus Dynasty (The Hidden History of Jesus, His Royal Family, and the Birth of Christianity)* (New York: Simon and Schuster, 2006). Refers to the entire book.

Notes to Chapter 1: The Movement Begins

2. Matthew 4:17
3. L. Michael White, *From Jesus to Christianity: How Four Generations of Visionaries & Storytellers Created the New Testament and Christian Faith* (New York: Harper Collins, 2004), 131.
4. Ibid.
5. Ibid., 123.
6. Williston Walker, *A History of the Christian Church*, (New York: Charles Scribner's Sons, 1959), 24.
7. Galatians 4:1–.
8. Romans 11:13,16.
9. Romans 14:17.
10. White, 159.
11. 1 Thessalonians 1:3, 9–10.
12. 1 Thessalonians 6.
13. I Thessalonians 4:1
14. 1 Thessalonians 4, 16-17.
15. 1 Corinthians 1:8.

16. 1 Corinthians 1:17.
17. 1 Corinthians 1:19.
18. Paul's letters raise the possibility that Gnosticism may have already existed in his time and that he may even have been influenced. First, he rejects strenuously "the wisdom of men" which may have referred to the Gnostic teachings attributed to Jesus. But he also uses "secret and hidden" (1 Corinthians 2:7) to characterize God's wisdom, an expression the Gnostics used to characterize their own wisdom. Even more suggestively, in Romans 8:3–6 he says, "God sent his own son *in the likeness of human flesh*," a very Gnostic and Docetic sounding expression.
19. 1 Corinthians 1:30.
20. 1 Corinthians 2:7.
21. Romans 1:3–4.
22. Romans 2:5.
23. Romans 1:18–20.
24. Romans 3:25.
25. Romans 4:24, 25.
26. Romans 4:3–5.
27. Romans 6:4.
28. Romans 8:3–6.
29. Romans 12:18–21.
30. Romans 12:2.
31. Romans 14:23.
32. Romans 16:25.
33. White, 157.
34. Ibid., 144.
35. Galatians 1:13a, 15–17.
36. Acts 22:6–8.
37. Galatians 2:11–14.
38. 1 Thessalonians 4:15–17a.
39. White, 218.

Notes to Chapter 2: The First Great Split
40. L. Michael White, *From Jesus to Christianity: How Four Generations of Visionaries & Storytellers Created the New Testament and Christian Faith* (New York: Harper Collins, 2004), 222–223.

41. James M. Robinson, *The Gospel of Jesus: In Search of the Original Good News*, (Harper Collins, 2005) p.29.

42. Plato taught that the natural world was merely a shadowy copy of the world of ideas. The Docetists, a non-Christian school of thought, adopted this view of what was real and what was not. Then the Gnostics picked up the idea and applied it to their teacher, Jesus. Therefore, for them, the physical Jesus was only an appearance of the real spiritual Jesus. So he did not suffer, nor did he really die, and those who learned and followed his teachings would be saved. That is, they would become, like Jesus, truly spiritual beings while their bodies became only appearances. Thus, the importance of Jesus as their teacher.

43. *The Apocalypse of Peter*, (a Gnostic document from the Nag Hammadi find), 79:22–31.

44. White, 465.

45. Ibid., 303. The name Thomas means "twin," and some have suggested that he was the twin of Jesus, but without any real evidence. However, the idea behind that suggestion was that Thomas was the real, physical reality while Jesus was the spiritual reality.

46. Robinson, 3.

47. Luke 19:12–13, 15–24; Matthew 25:14–15b, 19–20 and Thomas 41.

48. Luke 22:28, 30 and Matthew 19:28.

49. James D. Tabor, *The Jesus Dynasty (The Hidden History of Jesus, His Royal Family, and the Birth of Christianity)* (New York: Simon and Schuster, 2006). A reference to the book as a whole.

50. White, 134.

51. Robinson, 13.

52. Ibid., 14.

53. Luke 22:35–38.

54. Robinson, 14.

55. Ibid.

56. John Dominic Crossan, *Jesus: A Revolutionary Biography*, (New York: Harper Collins, 1995).

Notes to Chapter 3: What We Can Know and Can't

57. The first use of the term "Christianity" was by Ignasius circa 120 CE, in order to contrast it with Judaism.
58. *Newsweek*, June 27, 2005.
59. These criteria for historicity are fully discussed in Bart Ehrman's lectures on "The Historical Jesus" distributed by The Teaching Company.
60. Tacitus, *Annals*, 15–44.
61. Josephus, *Antiquities*, 18.63–64.
62. James D. Tabor, *The Jesus Dynasty (The Hidden History of Jesus, His Royal Family, and the Birth of Christianity)* (New York: Simon and Schuster, 2006). (The conclusion of the book's entire argument, no page number available).
63. L. Michael White, *From Jesus to Christianity: How Four Generations of Visionaries & Storytellers Created the New Testament and Christian Faith* (New York: Harper Collins, 2004), 102–105.
64. James M. Robinson, *The Gospel of Jesus: In Search of the Original Good News*, (New York: Harper Collins, 2005), 22.
65. Andrew Philip Smith, and Hoeller, Stephan A., *The Lost Sayings of Jesus*, (Vermont: Skylight Path Publishing, 2006), xviii.
66. *The Rutland Herald*, (Rutland, VT), July 2008, Section A4.
67. Michael Baigent, *The Jesus Papers: Exposing the Greatest Cover-up in History*, (San Francisco Harper, 2006).

Notes to Chapter 4: How the Church Tried to Define Him

68. Elaine Pagels, *The Gnostic Gospels*, (New York: Random House, 2004), 60.
69. Ibid., 104.
70. Armstrong, Karen. *The Bible: A Biography (Books That Changed the World)*, (New York: Atlantic Monthly Press, 2007), 1.
71. Ibid., 4.
72. Ibid.
73. Ibid., 102.
74. Ibid.
75. L. Michael White, *From Jesus to Christianity: How Four Generations of Visionaries & Storytellers Created the New Testament and Christian Faith* (New York: Harper Collins, 2004), 433.

Notes to Chapter 5: What Can We Do with Him Now?

76. Albert Schweitzer, *The Quest of the Historical Jesus*, (London: A&C Black Publishers, 1910), 401.
77. Jaroslav Pelikan, *Jesus Through the Centuries: His Place in the History of Culture*, (New York: Harper & Row, 1987).
78. The universal needs to which I refer are described in chapter seven of my book, *A New Vision of God for the 21st Century*, (Illinois: iUniverse Press, 2005). They are as follows: connection, hope, meaning, guidance, and understanding.
79. Erik Kolbell, *What Jesus Meant*, (Westminster John Knox Press, 2003), 12.
80. Joseph Campbell, *The Hero with a Thousand Faces*, (Bolling Foundation, 1949), 30.
81. "Light," as used in this title for Jesus, is a symbol suggested by my discussion of "spirit" in my book *A New Vision of God for the 21st Century*. "Light" and "darkness," as applied to the human and divine spirits in the chapter that follows, also represent the positive and negative aspects of spirit developed in the above cited book.

Notes to Chapter 7: Jesus for Today

82. Alighieri Dante, *The Divine Comedy*, (Connecticut: Grolier Enterprises Corp.,), 11.
83. The Acts of the Apostles 17:28.

Manufactured By: RR Donnelley
                     Breinigsville, PA USA
                     September, 2010